The Tibetan Book of the Dead, or *Bardo Todol*, is one of the great classics of Tibetan literature. The present volume is a fresh look at this timeless classic. It brings together a range of stunning images by the renowned photographer Thomas Kelly, with a contextual analysis and abridged translation by the ubiquitous Tibetologist Glenn H. Mullin.

As such, the *Bardo Todol* is as relevant as a guidebook to daily (and nightly) living as it is to a successful death and transmigration. Thomas Kelly's photographs bring this great Tibetan classic to life, and draw the reader into a deeper sense of the spiritual environment in which *The Tibetan Book of the Dead* exists.

Glenn H. Mullin has authored over two dozen books on Central Asian culture and is a consummate translator of classical Tibetan literature. Several of his titles have been translated into various European and Asian languages. He has also worked on Tibet-related films, including *Tibet: A Buddhist Trilogy*, and many television documentaries.

His book *The Fourteen Dalai Lamas: A Sacred Legacy of Reincarnation* was nominated for the NAPRA Best Book Award and *The Female Buddhas* won the Best Book Award from *Foreword Magazine*.

Thomas L. Kelly is an internationally recognized photographer who documents the beauty and grace of cultures in Southeast Asia and focuses on its two primary religions: Hinduism and Buddhism. He has researched and photographed over ten books based in South Asia and works avidly as a filmmaker and photo-activist, documenting the struggles of marginalized people and disappearing cultural traditions all over the world.

Kelly was named Photographer of the Year by *Hinduism Today* and his photos have been published in the *New York Times, Newsweek, Smithsonian* and *Time Magazine*.

The Tibetan Book of the Dead

The Tibetan Book of the Dead

An Illustrated Edition

PHOTOGRAPHS • THOMAS L. KELLY

TEXT • GLENN H. MULLIN

Lustre Press
Roli Books

Lord and Lady of the Charnel Grounds (Skt. Chitapati; Tib. Durdak). In ancient India, many tantric practitioners chose to meditate in graveyards and charnel grounds, partially as a reminder of impermanence and human frailty, but also for the fearsome nature of these sites, with the fear being used as a psychic stimulant. The image of the dancing Skeletal Lord and Lady was used as protection from wild animals and ghosts. This tangka painting was photographed in a monastery in Kham, Tibet, 1990.

Contents

Part One
The Tibetan Tradition of Life, Death and Transmigration

Following pages: *The theme of Chitapati (see caption to page 2) is often carried over into a monastic dance, or* tsam, *that is included in the annual festival of most Central Asian monasteries. One of the most popular* tsam *themes, the ritual invocation through dance of the* dharmapala, *or 'protector of truth,' involves monks dressed in costumes of the particular* dharmapalas *that are popular with their monastery. The dance usually lasts an entire day and some monasteries have performed as many as 100 different* dharmapala *dances in their annual festival.*

Here, one of the dancers leaps out of the temple. His partner (not in the photo) will soon follow him to the temple courtyard, and join in the playful Charnel Ground dance. Kathok Monastery Festival, Kham, Peyul, Tibet, 1991.

Part Two
A Condensed Translation of the Bardo Todol, or The Tibetan Book of the Dead

Preface

This volume is not a historical study of the art associated with *The Tibetan Book of the Dead,* nor of the Tibetan ideas on death and the after-death state. I dedicated an earlier book to this latter subject.[1] Rather, it is a re-contextualization of this great classic, and a preliminary expedition into the mystical land of bardo art.

It also is not a literal re-translation of the Tibetan text. Several versions already exist in English and these serve their purposes very well. Instead, Tom and I have attempted to throw a new perspective on this important work – he with his wonderful photographs, and me with the text accompanying these photos.

In Part One of the book I address the background of the Tibetan tradition on death and dying. In Part Two I create an abbreviated translation stripped of technical jargon.

A pilgrim performs prostrations at the famed Jonang Kumbum in Puntsokling, Tsang, Tibet. The monument is built in the form of a stupa (Tib. chorten*), symbolic of the enlightenment mind or* dharmakaya. *An early name for the Jonang Kumbum Chorten is Tongdrol Chenpo, or 'Great Liberation on Beholding'. The idea is that meditating in the presence of this sacred burial mound produces great inner transformation.*

In particular, I leave out the sections of the Tibetan text that enunciate the physical descriptions of the *Zhi Tro's Lha* or 'Peaceful and Wrathful Deities'. Although the recitation of these descriptions would be emotionally comforting for a Tibetan who chants the mandala manual daily, for most modern readers these descriptions only serve as a digression from the central meaning of the tradition.

I first encountered the *Bardo Todol* some forty years ago. It was one of the first books on Tibetan Buddhism that I had ever read, and it shook me to the very core of my being. I have owned a copy ever since. At the time I had no idea that I would go on to become a translator of Tibetan classical literature, nor that I would publish over two dozen of my own works on Tibetan Buddhism.

In an interview I once conducted with the present Dalai Lama, he commented that our world is in a delicate situation. He went on to mention the prophecies spoken by the Buddha in the *Kalachakra Tantra,* wherein Buddha speaks of the century beginning 2,500 years after his passing (officially recognized as 1956 by the international Buddhist community) as entering a crossroads phase. According to these prophecies, during this period humanity will create the basis for establishing either a thousand-year-long Golden Age, or a thousand years of darkness. 'For the former to occur,' His Holiness said, 'every community must offer the best of its accomplishments, and must leave behind the worst. This will create a reservoir of common human culture that can sustain the prophesied golden era.' His Holiness concluded by stating that Tibetans have four spheres of knowledge in which they can make significant contributions: meditation, practical neurology, cosmology, and medicine.

All four of these subjects are relevant to this book. Meditation quiets the mind and leads one's awareness to an understanding of impermanence, death, dying, and the after-death state. Practical neurology involves controlling brain chemistry and metabolism through Buddhist kundalini yoga, so that the actual death state can be simulated and fully experienced during meditation. Cosmology refers to the *Kalachakra* expression, 'As without, so within', wherein the body is understood as a microcosm of the universe, and the relationship between the physical and the mental/spiritual is revealed. Finally, Buddhist medicine involves the science of taking the first three of these four themes and applying them to the unfolding process of a human organism, so as to enhance health, harmony and balance. In the end, of course, the ultimate healing is enlightenment itself, and the attainment of what in Tibetan literature is referred to as *chimey yeshey*, 'the undying wisdom'.

The *Bardo Todol*, or *Tibetan Book of Liberation in the Bardo*, is perhaps the most internationally famous Tibetan text. Better known in the West as *The Tibetan Book of the Dead* because of the early translation by Kazi Samdup and Evans-Wentz, who gave their 1927 edition this name, it has seen numerous renditions into English over the years, and now exists in some form or another in well over a hundred languages worldwide.

Yet, even though much is known about the *Bardo Todol* as a classical work of Tibetan literature, very little is known about the visual world associated with it. Thus when Roli Books expressed an interest in bringing out an edition structured around photographs from the archives of my old friend Tom Kelly, and invited me to participate in the project, I was both delighted and honoured.

Hopefully the reader will find some pleasure and beauty in it. For although death and the after-death states do have something of a downside to them, they nonetheless – like all things in life – offer jewels of great power and wisdom.

Glenn H. Mullin
Ulaan Bataar, Mongolia

Part One

The Tibetan Tradition of Life, Death and Transmigration

Facing page: *A fresco painting of the Buddha on a temple wall in Mustang slowly fades and succumbs to the laws of impermanence. Dupa Village, Mustang, Nepal, 1991.*

Following pages: *Often misrepresented as the Sleeping Buddha, this statue shows the Buddha in the Lion Posture, which he showed on the day of his death. This image is one of the four main forms of the Buddha used in the great pilgrimage sites: those associated with his birth, his enlightenment, his first teaching, and his passing away. Here, a monk prays in front of the statue, an indication of the importance of the death theme in Buddhist meditation. Kushinagar, India, 1991.*

Chapter One

Death Awareness for a Happy Life

Facing page: *An elderly Buddhist nun. Everest region, Nepal, 2003.*

Following pages: *Himalayan yogis from Humla perform rituals on the banks of Lake Mansarovar, Tibet.*

Of all footprints in the forest,
That of the elephant is most large.
Of all contemplations, the contemplation of death
And impermanence has the strongest impact.

The Buddha in The Udanavarga

Buddha Shakyamuni considered a cultivated awareness of death and impermanence to be fundamental to a happy and healthy life.

It is often said that meditation upon death and impermanence was the first teaching the Buddha gave after his enlightenment, when he spoke of the four noble truths (suffering, its causes, liberation, and the path to liberation), because lack of awareness of impermanence and change is a principal cause of human suffering. Those who do not recognize the impermanent nature of phenomena develop superficial relationships with them, and live in emotional spheres based on delusion and fantasy. This in turn produces attachments and aversions, neither of which is conducive to inner happiness. These distorted emotions produce negative actions that bring frustration and unhappiness to oneself and others.

Facing page: *A monk contemplates his image in the mirror, as part of a meditation on how things appear to be real, but exist in a manner utterly different from their appearance. Just as the reflection seems substantial and solid, yet is merely a play of light that arises as an image in the mind. Dharamsala, India, 1991.*

Following pages: *The door of a temple portrays the Lord and Lady of the Charnel Grounds, as a reminder of impermanence and death. Negi Gompa, Kathmandu, Nepal, 1986.*

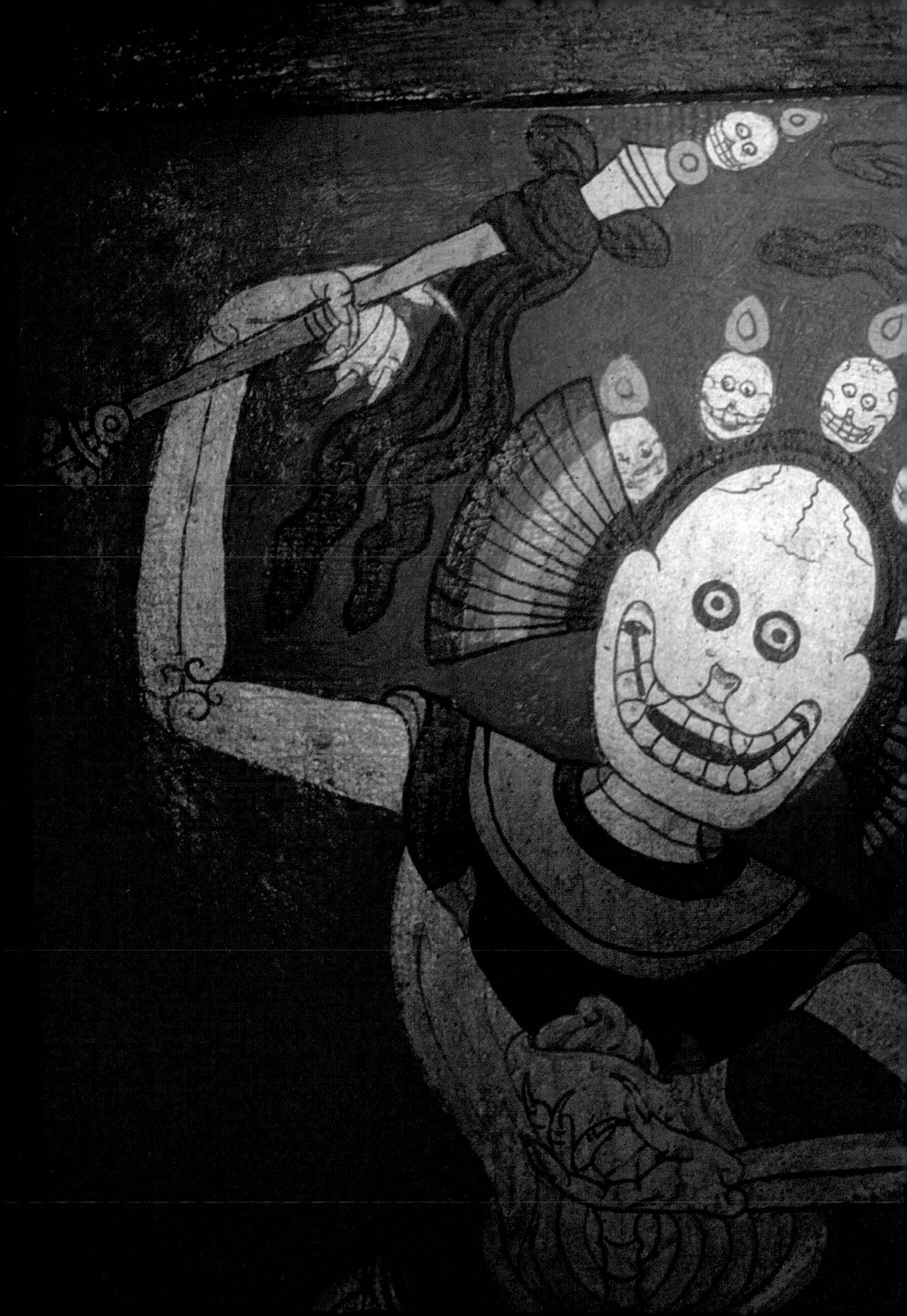

Conversely, awareness of impermanence and change is a primary element in turning the mind toward liberation. Because all things are impermanent, all personal faults can be transcended and all perfections achieved. As Buddha put it in *The Dharmapada,*

> All component things are impermanent.
> When one acquires realization of this truth
> One naturally releases the bonds of unhappiness.
> This is the way of purification and freedom.

Above: *An offering of light, surrounded by stones with mantras carved into them that represent various divine forms. The light symbolizes wisdom, the greatest aspect of the human spirit, a precious treasure that travels in this impermanent body vessel. Kathmandu, Nepal, 2007.*

The Kadampa lamas of eleventh-century Tibet, who based their contemplative tradition on the lineage of the Bengali master Atisha Dipamkara Shrijnana, said that if one does not contemplate death and impermanence upon waking in the morning, the entire morning will lose its strength; if one does not contemplate it at noon, the afternoon will be squandered; and if one does not contemplate it in the evening, the night will be similarly lost.[1]

This meditation on death and impermanence is not a morbid fascination or indulgence, but is practised in the context of the joy of positive living. It is the other side of the coin of celebration. For this reason the Kadampa lamas would begin their meditation sessions with a contemplation of *milu rinpoche*, 'the precious nature of human life': the belief that achieving human rebirth is as rare and precious as finding a wish-fulfilling gem.

In a commentary to this Kadampa tradition the First Dalai Lama (1391-1475) wrote, 'The Kadampa lamas recommend that one meditate on the preciousness of one's human life until one's eyes fill with tears of joy.' He went on to say, 'Only then should one proceed to the contemplations of death and impermanence: on how death is inevitable, how its time is uncertain, and on how at the time of death the only possessions of value are the inner jewels of the spirit.'

The Fifth Dalai Lama (1617-1682) expresses the same sentiment in verse in his *Instructions of Manjushri*:[2]

> This precious human life, a boat that can carry us
> To higher wisdom and eternal happiness,
> Has only now been gained. If we do not use it
> To travel to the jewel island of enlightenment,
> And instead allow ourselves to die empty-handed,
> Are the very veins of our heart not corroded?

And the Second Dalai Lama (1475-1542) also wrote in a poem to a disciple,[3]

This human life with its freedoms and endowments
Is a supreme vessel for spiritual training.
Think over the precious opportunity that is yours
And take advantage of it, Jampel Drak . . .
Do not leave yourself armed only with regret
When the Lord of Death strikes, Jampel Drak.

Just as death and impermanence was Buddha's first teaching, it was also his final one. Some forty-five years after his enlightenment he announced that he had completed his life's work, and requested that his principal disciples meet him in Kushinigar to be with him during his final days. On the day of his passing he delivered a final discourse to the gathering, entered meditation, and with full awareness departed from this world.

As we will see later in this book, the Buddhist tradition regards meditation on death and impermanence not only as a useful technique for keeping the mind intensely focused; it also sees it as a method for unlocking the deepest secrets of life. This is especially true in the Buddhist tantric legacy, which involves yoga for death simulation. The bodily processes are stilled, and the heartbeat and breathing slowed to imperceptible levels. Consciousness is separated from its physical base, and the meditator is then able to enter directly into the after-death state in meditation for hours and even days at a time, returning to the body when the session is complete. The Seventh Dalai Lama (1708-1757) expresses this in a verse,[4]

The outer consort, in nature fire,
Melts the life drops that course
Through the 72,000 channels,
Bringing them into the central channel and
Giving rise to the four ineffable delights.

Outside, all sensory movements of mind and energy cease;
Inside, mundane views, ignorance and darkness disperse.

Tangka of the wisdom dakini *Vajra Varahi. Karsha Monastery, Zanskar, India, 1994.*

In this way through tantric yoga sleep is transformed
Into the nature of *dharmakaya's* pure light and
The very experience of the beyond-death state aroused . . .

Thus during this very life death itself is experienced
And the beyond-death wisdom is achieved.

The *Bardo Todol,* or *The Tibetan Book of the Dead,* is part of this tradition of living one's life with an awareness of death in order to maintain a maximum intensity of spiritual presence. It is also part of the tradition of understanding or experiencing the after-death state in meditation during this lifetime by means of tantric application.

Facing page top: *A lama in retreat in his mountainside hermitage. Humla, Nepal, 1990.*
Below: *A newborn Tibetan child lies in a sheepskin bed, and the cycle begins again. Gyanste, Tibet, 1990.*

Following pages: *Modern wall fresco depicting Buddha at the time of his death, surrounded by his principal disciples. Sarnath, India, 1990.*

Chapter Two

Reincarnation and the Wheel of Becoming

Fresco painting of the Wheel of Becoming, with everything held between the jaws of Yama, the Lord of Death. Dharamsala, India, 1990.

The Tibetan Book of the Dead makes repeated mention of 'The Six Realms of Existence'. An entire section of the text is dedicated to instructions on how to close the doors to these six realms.[1]

The six realms can be spoken of on outer, inner and secret levels. On an outer level they are realms of rebirth; on an inner level they are six states of mind in which the nature of the self is misunderstood; and on a secret level they are subtle energy dynamics within our chakra and *nadi* energy system.

The Tibetan Book of the Dead is mostly concerned with the outer and inner meanings, simply because anyone who has mastered the secret meaning will not require assistance at the time of death. This is clearly stated in an introductory passage of the text,[2]

This method for mediocre yogis to gain liberation in the bardo,
The great text for achieving liberation through hearing,

Bhutanese pilgrim offering devotion in front of a fresco of Avalokiteshvara, the Buddha of Compassion. His 1,000 eyes watch and 1,000 hands uplift and rescue both during life and during death/transmigration.

Is presented in three sections:
The foreword; the actual text; and the afterword.

As for the first of these, the foreword, here it is said
That those of superior capacity – the great yogis –
    should gain liberation
During this very lifetime by relying on the stages of practice.
If they do not succeed in this, then they should apply
The methods of consciousness at the time of death.

Even mediocre yogis can gain liberation in this way.
However, if they do not succeed in the effort,
Then they should turn to a reading of this text,
For achieving liberation through hearing in the bardo.

Most Tibetans think of the six realms primarily as places of reincarnation. The idea is that a person dies and then takes rebirth in one of the six, depending on the driving forces of karma and delusion. As the Seventh Dalai Lama put it in a verse,[3]

Bad karma and delusion:
Evil spirits riding upon the horse of the mind,
Corroding the very thread of life.
Carried helplessly along by them,
This life is made short and the next destitute . . .
Thus bad karma generates more bad karma
As we wander through the six realms of existence.

Facing page: *A lama circumambulates around Mount Kailash, the most sacred site in the Hindu and Buddhist worlds. The mountain is a metaphor for the axis at the centre of the universe, and a pilgrimage around it purifies the mind of the six delusions associated with the six realms. Western Tibet, 1987.*

Following pages: *Cremation of a high Tibetan refugee lama, Urgyen Tulku. In accordance with tradition, the body is seated in the meditation posture, dressed in the costume of tantric self-empowerment, and placed inside a special stupa-shaped pyre. After the cremation, the stupa is dismantled and scattered into all directions, as a way of blessing the world. Nepal, 1996.*

And also,[4]

This life, flowing constantly like a mountain stream,
Pauses not for a moment;
It ends within a century, when body and mind part ways.
Will the Lord of Death not come to you too?

At that time only one's karmic imprints follow
As Death leads one away. Look now to what you will do then,
When alone and friendless you must enter
The great path of the bardo, that long and treacherous pass.
If at that time you have not gained liberation,
Then again you must take uncontrolled rebirth in the six realms.

These six realms are often depicted in a painting known in Tibetan as *Sipai Khorlo,* or the 'Wheel of Life', in which a large globe is held in the mouth of Yama, the Lord of Death (*see* page 32). When one looks closely within the globe one notices various hell realms at the bottom, heavenly realms above and the realms of ghosts, animals and man in between.

The symbolism of the six realms being held in the jaws of Yama is that all six are subject to the laws of impermanence and change and, in the end, to death and rebirth. As the Second Dalai Lama put it in a poem to a female disciple,[5]

The Lord of Death indiscriminately devours
All beings of the six realms.

The entranceway to most Tibetan temples has a fresco of this image. The idea is that turning to enlightenment is the only way to go beyond the six realms.

An entire book could be written on the Wheel of Life, for it contains keys to many of the fundamental Buddhist doctrines, illustrating both how we wander in samsara and how we accomplish enlightenment.

Lama in his meditation cave. Humla, Nepal, 1986.

The painting is called a 'wheel' because it has an outer rim, a hub at the centre and various spokes connecting the two. The outer rim is divided into twelve segments. These represent what Buddhists call 'the twelve links of dependent origination'. The meaning is that everything we do sets in motion a sequence of events that unfold as cause-and-effect phenomena. Conversely, everything we experience is a culmination or ripening of previous causes and effects.

The first of the links usually shows a man with an arrow in his eye. The arrow is ignorance of the nature of the self. This ignorance blinds us, causing us to create unenlightened karma that eventually produces rebirth in one of the six realms of cyclic existence. Even if the realm is a happy one, the happiness is limited and eventually transforms into suffering and death. This is symbolized by the last of the twelve links, which shows old age and death.

The hub of the wheel usually contains several different images. At the centre of the hub we see a rooster, snake and pig chasing one another in circles. These three animals represent attachment, anger and ignorance, the three root delusions. These delusions support and intensify one another.

Outside of this we usually see a circle of humans. Those on the right are painted in darkness, and show a line of people being pulled downward. Those on the left are painted in light and are being led upward, usually by monks or by a buddha figure. The meaning is that the three root delusions pull us down into deep suffering, whereas the ways of enlightenment lead us upward, toward liberation and happiness.

A number of spokes – usually five or six – connect the hub of the wheel to the rim. The six realms are depicted in the areas between the spokes: the hells at the bottom; the realms of ghosts, animals and human beings on the sides; and the realms of fighting gods and higher gods above.

The Tibetan Book of the Dead is very much concerned with these six realms as actual places of rebirth. Its aim is to inspire the deceased to avoid reincarnating in them, and instead to achieve liberation and enlightenment.

All schools of Tibetan Buddhism take great delight in describing the nature of life in the six realms of worldly existence. Spiritual training in all schools begins with contemplating them and the karmic causes resulting in rebirth within them.

Traditional scriptures speak of eight hot hells, eight cold hells, and various surrounding and occasional hells. These are often depicted individually in Wheel of Life paintings. The scriptures also speak of many different god realms.

The three lower realms are often termed *ngen-dro sum*, or 'three realms of misery', while the three upper ones are called *den-dro sum*, or 'three pleasant realms'. However, all six are equally undesirable. The three higher realms might be temporarily more pleasant than the lower three, but in the end the person dies and falls again. The Seventh Dalai Lama expresses it this way,

> Even in the blissful abodes of the desire gods,
> Where the mind is bound in unconscious indulgence,
> The signs of death eventually manifest
> And cause suffering followed by a fall.[6]

The three animals at the centre of the hub that represent the three delusions are sometimes made to represent six. These are the six primary *klesha* or distorted states of mind as listed in the *abhidharma* literature.[7]

The Tibetan Book of the Dead makes a direct link between these six primary *klesha* and the six realms of worldly existence. The realms of the gods are associated with pride and self-complacency; the realm of the titans is linked to jealousy and envy; the human realm with arrogance and egotism; the ghost realms are associated with greed and attachment; the animal realms with unconscious and instinctual living; and finally, the hells are associated with anger and violence.

This is the inner interpretation of the Wheel of Life. Humans oscillate between these six negative mental states and in doing so they flip from realm to realm in their mental and emotional lives. The feeling of anger is itself hell; the feeling of attachment and craving is itself the ghost realm; and so forth.

The Tibetans did not invent this way of looking at the six realms, but rather inherited it from India. For example, the sixth-century Indian master

Shantideva writes in his magnum opus, *A Guide to the Bodhisattva Way,*[8]

> Who fashioned the torture instruments of the hells
> And the terrible situations of the ghost realms?
> Verily they are produced by one's own inner processes:
> By one's inner energies and delusions.

Paintings of the Wheel of Life often depict a buddha standing in the upper-right corner. He is pointing to an image in the upper left. This second image can be a buddhafield, a dharma wheel, or a buddha or bodhisattva. The meaning is that we transcend ordinary birth and death by means of application to the dharma, the path leading to liberation and enlightenment. The sentiment is expressed by a passage in *The Tibetan Book of the Dead,*

> Kyema! Out of unconscious karmic instinct I now wander in
> samsara.
> May the radiance of the primordial innate free me from all fear.
> O peaceful and wrathful deities, lead the way.
> O supreme consorts and great *dakinis,* hold me from behind.
> Show me how to cross the terrible path of the bardo.
> Point the way to the state of buddhahood itself.
>
> When countless empty images appear as peaceful and wrathful
> forms
> May the buddhas hold me with the hooks of their compassion.
> When the five great radiances arise,
> May I recognize them as my own mental projections.
> When the peaceful and wrathful deities appear,
> May I remain strong and without fear.
>
> When the force of my own negative karma brings pain,
> May my mandala practice hold me free.
> When great thunderous sounds arise in the bardo,

May I hear only *om mani padme hum,* the mantra of compassion.

May I rely upon Avalokiteshvara, Buddha of Compassion.
May I rely upon samadhi, the meditation on inseparable bliss
and void.
May I see the five elements as friends, and not as enemies.
May I see right now the realms of the five buddhas.

Above: *Preparing a corpse for a sky funeral, Tibet, late nineteenth century.*

Following pages: *Tibetan pilgrims prostrate in front of the Jhokang Temple. Lhasa, Tibet, 1991.*

Chapter Three

The Tibetan Book of the Dead and the Three Ways to Enlightenment

Fourteenth century painting of Padma Sambhava, the inspiration behind The Tibetan Book of the Dead. *He is flanked by his Indian disciple/lover Mandarava and Tibetan disciple/lover Yeshey Tsogyal, and surrounded by lineage gurus and tantric deities. (© John Gilmore Ford Family Collection)*

Indian classical Buddhist literature speaks of three different aspects of the Buddha's teachings: Hinayana, Mahayana and Vajrayana, or Compact Way, Universal Way and Diamond Way. The first of the three emphasizes individual liberation, the second emphasizes universal love and compassion, and the third emphasizes power and quick realization.

The first two are often grouped together and termed Sutrayana, or Way of the Public Discourses, for Buddha taught them in public forums to large audiences. The third is then called Guhyamantrayana, or Way of the Secret Mantra, for it was taught in secrecy to small groups of *mantrikas,* or tantric yogis.

The nature of meditation practice in each of the Three Ways is also very different. In general it is said that the methods of the first two work with conventional levels of consciousness and require many lifetimes of

Facing page: *Monks in prayer during a tantric festival led by the Dalai Lama. Bodh Gaya, India, 1990.*

Following pages: *Pilgrims circumambulating a sand mandala of the Kalachakra Tantra, or 'Mystery of the Wheel of Time', during a ceremonial initiation led by the Dalai Lama. Dharamsala, India, 1996.*

effort for the attainment of liberation and enlightenment, whereas the third level works with the unconventional level of consciousness and brings easy enlightenment within one lifetime.

In ancient India a practitioner would often choose one or another of the Three Ways and stick with it. As the centuries passed, however, it became more common to unite all three within one's training regime, and by the seventh and eighth centuries, when Buddhism became the national religion of Tibet, this unified approach was more the norm than the exception. Some other Buddhist countries and lineages have opted for a more specialized application, and continue the earlier way of keeping the three as distinct entities.

The Buddha taught many different systems within the Vajrayana. Each has its own *Mulatantra*, or Root Scripture, as well as a mandala that is unique to the transmission. Each also has its own unique purpose and principal feature, as well as its own initiation ceremony, lineage of transmission, daily practice system, retreat procedure, and associated rituals. With the passing of generations, each also accumulated its own body of literature.

Many tantric systems are known by the name of their chief mandala deity or buddha form, although most mandalas have numerous deities, sometimes even hundreds. Numerous meditations and mantras are associated with each of these mandala deities.

In the early days, most of the individual tantric systems were kept separate from one another, and each was regarded as a complete path to enlightenment. But here again the passage of time brought about fusion and cross-fertilization, and a tradition of uniting the various tantras emerged, at least on a simple level for daily meditation. This was very common with the lower tantras, where a tradition of trinities became popular.

The greatest fusion, however, did not occur in India, but in Tibet, with the appearance of the 'Mandala of 100 Peaceful and Wrathful Deities'. The exact history of this development is yet to be written, but the idea

Fresco of the Buddha, the ultimate source of the Buddhist teachings on the bardo. Patan, Nepal, 1986.

behind the structure is probably connected to the old Mongolian shamanic tradition of a 'Circle of 100 Black and White Deities', all of whom fall under the jurisdiction of the supreme 'Eternal Blue Sky'. This shamanic tradition had spread through Tibet and the Himalayas from the time of Mongolia's Khunna (i.e. Hun) empire in the third and second centuries BC, if not earlier.[1]

The ancient Tibeto-Mongolian shamanic tradition provided an excellent working basis for Tantric Buddhism. The two easily fit together both philosophically and in terms of basic practice. The many peaceful and wrathful deities of the Buddhist tantras adapted themselves within the shamanic infrastructure.

The actual work of directing this fusion and the emergence of this eclectic Buddhist mandala is usually attributed to the eighth-century

Above: *A Buddhist stupa, or sacred burial mound, in Anaradapuram, Sri Lanka, 1996.*

Facing page: *Sipai Gyalmo, or 'Queen of the Universe', a* dharmapala *common to both Bonpo and Buddhist traditions. She rides in a fire of wisdom over an ocean of raging blood. Triten Norbutse Monastery, Kathmandu, Nepal, 1991.*

subcontinental master Padma Sambhava, who was born in Uddiyana (modern-day Swat in Pakistan) on the old silk and spice trade routes. At the time, Uddiyana was a stopover Buddhist trading centre between India, China, Persia and Europe. Thus it was a hotbed of the ideas that travelled with the caravans and traders.

After growing up in this very international environment, Padma Sambhava went to central India for higher Buddhist education. Later he was invited to Tibet by King Trisong Deutsan. How many of Padma Sambhava's legendary accomplishments are historically true, and how many are born from the fertile Tibetan imagination, has been a hotly-debated subject among Tibetan scholars for centuries. However, there is a unanimous agreement that he was the vehicle of great developments in Tibet and Tibetan Buddhism. Whether all of these were done by him personally, or were done by others in his name, is not especially important.

It is important that at this time the tradition of a Mandala of 100 Peaceful and Wrathful Deities emerged as a fusion of many different Indian Buddhist tantric systems, perhaps inspired by Padma Sambhava's encounter with the ancient Tibeto-Mongolian shamanic legacy of a Circle of 100 Black and White Deities.

As we will see later, it is this Mandala of 100 Peaceful and Wrathful Deities that became the basis of the visionary text known as the *Bardo Todol* or *The Tibetan Book of the Dead.*

Padma Sambhava also encouraged the classical Indian tradition of practising the Three Ways of the Buddha as an integrated approach, with the Hinayana used as the basis, the Mahayana as the overall structure, and the Vajrayana as the finishing adornment. The *Bardo Todol* takes the language of the Vajrayana as its principal environment, but very much incorporates the ideas and sentiments of the other two Ways.

Facing page: *Meditator holding a ritual bell, symbol of feminine wisdom. Humla, Nepal, 1986.*

Following pages: *Buddhist monk performing rituals to heal those stuck in the bardo. Pokhara, Nepal, 1986.*

Chapter Four

Indian Mahasiddhas and the Charnel Grounds Culture

Indian mahasiddha *Jalandhara with his tantric consort. The* mahasiddhas *abandoned monastic life for the more exotic life of forest yoga, usually with a sexual partner. Dharamsala, India, 1990.*

Each of the Three Ways to Enlightenment discussed in the previous chapter has its own hero or role model. The role model in the Hinayana is the *arhat,* who has eliminated all karma and delusions and achieved the liberation of nirvana. In the Mahayana tradition the model is the bodhisattva, the altruistic practitioner who strives to achieve omniscient buddhahood as a means of benefitting all living beings. Finally, the model in the Vajrayana is the tantric *mahasiddha,* who lives fearlessly in terrifying places such as remote jungles and charnel grounds.

In Buddhist art the *arhat* is usually depicted as a monk, for the monastic vows are in the category of Hinayana teachings and the bodhisattva is often depicted as a princely lay person, for many of the Mahayana teachings were given to lay practitioners. Finally, the tantric *mahasiddha* is often depicted as a half-naked and half-mad yogi, with long unkempt hair, an unwashed body, and ornaments made from human bones.

Facing page: *A Tibetan yogi uses a* kangling, *or human thighbone trumpet, as well as a large hand drum, in a ritual to liberate wandering souls. Derge, Tibet, 1990.*

Following pages: *Tangka detail, perhaps eighteenth century: Animals feed on corpses left in a charnel ground. A Tibetan monastery, 2001.*

The Buddhist fascination with charnel grounds began with Buddha himself. In ancient India most towns and cities chose a site near the forest or jungle where they would place the corpses of deceased people. Some would be cremated, but most would choose the charnel grounds as their final destination. Here their bodies would be laid out in the fresh air, and left to serve as food offerings to wild animals and birds. This was a final act of charity on the part of the deceased – having eaten all of his or her life, the dead person would now be food for others. Relatives would often come and make token offerings of food and clothing to the spirit of the deceased, as a way of dealing with personal grief and as a means of generating closure in the relationship.[1]

In the early days of Buddhism a monk was often instructed to fashion his own robes by taking clothes of the dead from the charnel grounds and dying them with saffron. This helped the dead person gather merit by creating a karmic link with a meditator, and also helped remind the monk

Above: *Pilgrims offering tribute in a temple. Lubrok, Mustang, 1991.*

Facing page: *Village lamas perform death rituals at a cremation ceremony. Humla, Nepal, 1986.*

of the reality of death and impermanence. Monks were also instructed to meditate in the charnel grounds for a period and observe the various stages of the decomposition of a corpse, as a means of enhancing awareness of the truth of personal mortality.

Over the centuries, however, Buddha's idea of the monk as a wandering mendicant gradually faded and was replaced by a more sedentary vision. The hundreds of small *viharas* that dotted the Indian landscape, where wandering Buddhist mendicants could stay for a few days or rest during the rainy season, were replaced with large, comfortable monasteries where a monk could live his entire life. This sedentary life also offered an increased ability to gather and store possessions, and the tradition of making robes from rags found in charnel grounds was replaced with making them from cloth offered by family and friends. By the fourth and fifth centuries, the charnel ground culture had been more or less abandoned by the monastics.

It was at this time that the tantric *mahasiddhas* began to appear. Like the early Buddhist monks, they too spent much of their time in charnel grounds, where they ate the food and wore the clothing left for the dead. However, they did not take the monastic precepts, and often engaged in behaviour that was in clear contradiction of the monk code, especially sexual activity and the consumption of alcohol. To symbolize this, they are sometimes depicted as sitting in sexual union with a consort, with a jug of wine somewhere to the side or with a consort or two standing in the background.

Although there were thousands of charnel grounds in ancient India and most villages had one within a few hours of walking distance, eight large ones were considered especially significant, and became known as the 'eight great charnel grounds'. Many *mahasiddhas* travelled to all eight at one time or another in their lives in order to meditate in them.[2]

Besides being auspicious places for tantric meditation, charnel grounds were also popular sites for the bimonthly tantric feast, which is performed on the tenth and twenty-fifth days of the lunar cycle. During these two days the energies of the body are said to become especially subtle and a spiritual

Yogambhara, a tantric 'male-female in union' meditational deity. Date of painting is uncertain. Nepal, 1996.

epiphany is most easily attained. Consequently, during these two days, male and female tantric practitioners would often gather in the charnel grounds and celebrate a *ganachakra*, or tantric feast, consuming large quantities of meat and alcohol. These feasts often involved sexual orgies of various levels of intensity.

In later centuries the monastic community managed to wrestle the tantric tradition away from the *mahasiddhas* and bring it into the puritanical world of celibate monkhood. The large quantities of meat and alcohol of the *ganachakra* feasts was replaced by the tradition of consuming a tiny piece of meat, with a single drop of alcohol on a fingertip. The sexual orgies were replaced by visualizing oneself as a tantric buddha sitting in union with his female buddha consort. This is obviously not as much fun as the real thing, nor true to the spirit of Tantric Buddhism that the Indian *mahasiddhas* had embodied; but at least it has preserved the essence of the tradition in a symbolic manner.[3]

Because most of the Buddhist tantras were transmitted in early India through these lay *mahasiddhas* and not through the monastic community, and because most of the *mahasiddhas* became associated with the charnel grounds, many tantric mandalas have an outer ring depicting the eight great charnel grounds of India, with a *mahasiddha* sitting in each.[4]

Although Tibet's cold and dry climate did not lend itself well to the charnel ground method of body offering, and the Tibetans did not adopt the practice in the manner it was maintained in India, they did replace it with something quite similar: the *ja tor,* or bird offering, which is often termed 'sky burial' in Western literature. Most Tibetan towns had a *ja tor* site where dead bodies would be taken. Here a special class of yogis would cut them into small pieces and arrange these as a feast for the birds. The entire process was performed ritually, often beginning with a tantric dance and an invocation of the *dakinis,* or 'angelettes'.

The sound would call in the vultures, which would stand in a circle around the site until the preparations were complete. Flesh would be stripped from bone and cut into manageable niblets. Then the vital organs would be pounded into mush with a giant pestle, mixed with roasted barley flour, and formed into balls. Sometimes, even bones would be ground to powder and mixed with flour, although more often bones and hair would be cremated at the conclusion of the rite.

Above: *Raksha Tal, symbolic of wrathful female energy, embraces Gurla Mandata Mountain. Tibet, 1991.*

Following pages: *Two relatives look on as the corpse of their loved one is offered to the birds, and the soul is directed towards a buddha-field. Drigung, Tibet, 1990.*

When all was complete and the feast made ready in this way, the master of the rite would signal the birds to join in. The entire body would then be devoured in a matter of minutes.

This interpretation of the charnel ground suited the Tibetan climate better than the Indian method. India's heat would cause a body to break down within a matter of hours, and the strongly pungent smell to call animals from far and wide. Thus simply laying a body on the ground would be sufficient to achieve the desired effect. The cold of Tibet, however, did not afford this condition, for the body would simply freeze and turn into a block of ice. Thus the Indian method was replaced with the *ja tor*. Just as charnel grounds had served as favoured places of meditation for tantriks in India, these *ja tor* were similarly used for meditation by Tibetan yogis and tantric practitioners. However, because the Buddhist tantras had come from India, the Indian charnel grounds rather than the *ja tor* continued to be used in Tibetan art.

When China first opened Tibet to tourism in the 1980s, *ja tor* sites were put on the itineraries of many tourist groups. The large site outside of Lhasa just below Pabongkha offers a half-dozen or more bodies a day, and the famous one at Drigung is almost as busy. However, Tibetans found the gawking and constant clicking of cameras to be extremely offensive, so a greater respect and more appropriate sense of sanctity is observed these days.

The Tibetan Book of the Dead is very much an expression of this Indian *mahasiddha* culture, which was so deeply inspired by the Buddhist Tantras, for it is based on the Mandala of 100 Peaceful and Wrathful Deities, all of which are associated with the tantras. It can also be viewed as an expression of the charnel ground culture, with its concordant knowledge of death and the after-death states.

Tangka painting of the female buddha Vajrayogini drinking blood from a skull cup symbolizing the impermanence of human existence. Karsha Monastery, Zanskar, India, 1988.

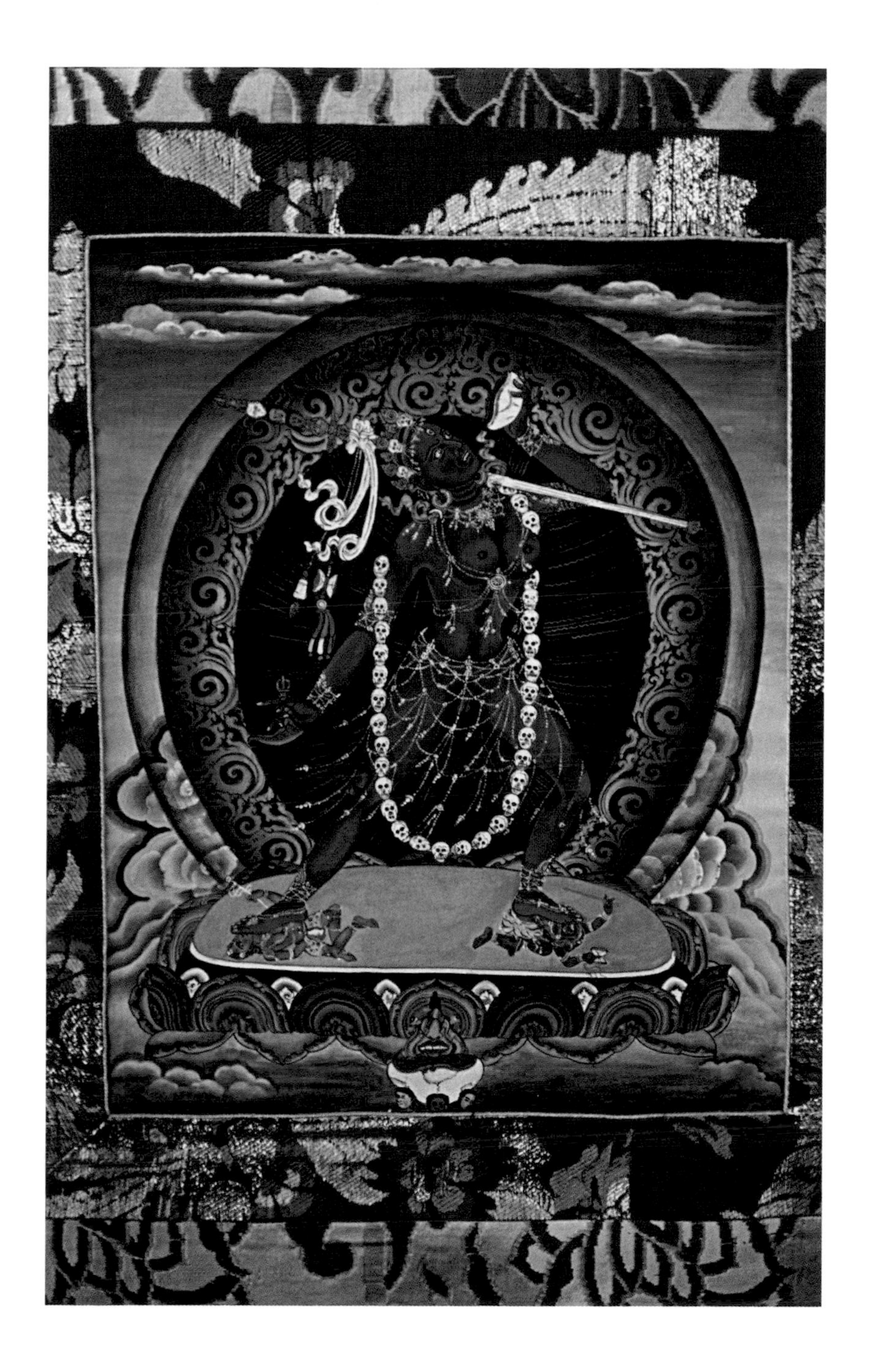

Chapter Five

The Tibetan Book of the Dead and the Bardo literature of Buddhist India

Facing page: *Monks chanting in front of the Mahabodhi Stupa in Bodh Gaya, where the Buddha manifested his enlightenment.*

Following pages: *Young refugee monks chanting Buddhist texts. Dharamsala, India, 1990.*

Although *The Tibetan Book of the Dead* is essentially a tantric scripture, it is nonetheless deeply informed by the Three Ways of Enlightenment taught by the Buddha.

On the Hinayana level, Buddhist literature is divided into three categories: *vinaya,* sutra and *abhidharma.* The essence of the first is self-discipline; the essence of the second is meditation; and the essence of the third is wisdom or philosophical training.

The subject of the death and after-death experiences is discussed in detail in the *abhidharma* category of literature. Of course Buddha himself is the most important source of this literature, but because he taught over a period of forty-five years after his enlightenment, the treatises by later Indian masters became important as study tools. These masters extracted the essence of Buddha's teachings on particular themes from the various sutras and arranged them by writing them in shastra form, or treatises for systematic study.

A tsam *dance in Triten Norbutse Monastery, Kathmandu, Nepal.*

The fourth-century masters Asanga and Vasubandhu became the two most important Indian writers dedicated to the work of compiling the *abhidharma* doctrines. The two shastras by them – the *Abhidharma-samucchaya* (*Compendium of Abhidharma*) by Asanga and the *Abhidharma-kosha* (*Treasury of Abhidharma*) by Vasubandhu – became the most important Sutrayana treatises for the study of the *abhidharma* topics. Consequently these two are also very important Sutrayana sources of the bardo information on which *The Tibetan Book of the Dead* is based. These two *abhidharma* works are studied by almost all Tibetan lamas. At the time *The Tibetan Book of the Dead* emerged, in the fourteenth century, a study of them was fundamental to all schools.

The *abhidharma* literature of the Hinayana and that of the Mahayana is much the same in terms of its discussion of death and after-death states.[1] However, a far greater clarity of detail emerges with the tantric tradition, especially the *maha-anuttara*-yoga-tantra, or 'Great Highest Yoga Tantra Systems'. Although, the old (Nyingma) and new (Sarma) schools of Tibetan Buddhism classify these Highest Yoga Tantra Systems slightly differently, and every sect favours specific mandala systems from India, the essence of all of them is much the same in terms of practice and essential doctrines.

All, for example, involve a first stage of application that is largely mandala visualization, and incorporates some form of the yoga known as 'taking the three occasions as the three kayas'. This involves the clear light of death as the formless *dharmakaya* of a buddha; the visions of the bardo – or after-death process of unfoldment – as the *sambhogakaya* of a buddha; and the re-emergence of rebirth as a buddha's *nirmanakaya*. These three ordinary experiences are brought into the structure of a mandala meditation, and visualized as taking on the complete qualities of the three kayas.

This mandala-based process of visualization is used to enhance the powers of meditation until some level of samadhi is attained. The yogi then proceeds to the second stage of practice, known as 'the completion

Facing page: *The yogi Milarepa with guru Marpa above, his chief disciple Gampopa off to the side, and lesser disciples below.*

Following pages: *Buddhist nuns at Negi Gompa blow conch shells at dawn, to summon the community for its morning devotions. Nepal, 1987.*

stage', wherein these three 'occasions' are actually generated in meditation by means of the chakra, *nadi* and prana practices of *chandali* (or kundalini) yoga.[2]

Although each tantric system has its own way of presenting the tantric yogas, the second-century Indian master Nagarjuna's tradition of speaking about five basic completion-stage applications is somewhat pervasive, with the five being as follows: yogas for stilling bodily energies, yogas for stilling emotional and discursive energies, illusory body yogas, clear light yogas, and great union yogas. Various tantric systems might use other names or structures, but the processes come down to these five.

All five of these levels of training deal with extracting the mind from ordinary levels of experience and moving it toward the primordial clear light consciousness, which is similar to the clear light of death. After the clear light is aroused, the process is reversed on subtle levels and the after-death bardo dimension is experienced in meditation.[3]

As mentioned earlier, although in the early days of Tantric Buddhism each system was taught and practised individually, the passage of generations saw a tendency to fuse the different systems.

One of the most important Indian masters in this process of lineage fusion was the great Tilopa, who appeared in the tenth century. He gathered many different tantric systems and then reorganized their salient yogic features into an integrated methodology for application. Later he passed his lineages to Naropa, who gave them to the Tibetan mystic Marpa the translator. Marpa transmitted them to the great yogi Milarepa, and from him they came down through numerous lines in the tradition known as 'The Six Yogas of Naropa'. Naropa gave a slightly different version of these six yogas to his female disciple Niguma, and her Tibetan disciple Khyungpo Naljor in the tradition known as 'The Six Yogas of Niguma.'

An important element common to both of these transmissions became famous as bardo *naljor*, or 'yoga for the bardo state'. Another was *milam naljor*,

A monk performs a 'mandala offering', a ritual symbolic of transforming the universe into a buddha-field, and dedicating it to enlightenment. He makes a gesture with his fingers that represent Mt Meru at the centre and the four continents in the four directions. Bodh Gaya, India, 1990.

or 'yoga for the dream state'. Both are systems of meditation practised in conjunction with the *chandali* (illusory) body and clear light yogas. Tilopa extracted the bardo teachings from numerous tantric systems, and arranged all the various doctrines and yogic techniques into a simple and coherent approach for easy study and practice and for quick attainment of realization.

Often dream yoga and bardo yoga are mentioned together, because the tantras state that the dream body is very similar to the bardo body. For this reason it is sometimes said that success in bardo yoga depends upon success in dream yoga. We will examine more about these two in a later section.

Suffice it to say here that there is a good probability that the dream and bardo yogas of the two systems of Six Yogas descending from Naropa played a significant role in the formulation of *The Tibetan Book of the Dead*. Three centuries passed between the time that Marpa and Khyungpo Naljor brought their Six Yogas systems to Tibet, and these systems had by then become widespread in all schools of Tibetan Buddhism, including the Nyingma. There is no doubt that when Karma Lingpa presented *The Tibetan Book of the Dead* in the late fourteenth century, well over 300 years after these lineages of the Six Yogas had become known in every corner of the country, he did so with full awareness of the bardo teachings of the Indian *mahasiddhas* Tilopa and Naropa that came to Tibet through Marpa Lotsawa and Khyungpo Naljor.

We will see more of the Marpa lineages of 'the three blendings', and their relevance to the doctrines of *The Tibetan Book of the Dead*. In brief, however, it is safe to say that *The Tibetan Book of the Dead* is a theatrical replaying of the bardo yogas, set within the context of the Mandala of 100 Peaceful and Wrathful Deities.[4]

A meditation chamber with shrunken human heads. Tibet, 1920.

Chapter Six

Bardo, Dreams, Sex and Death

Facing page: *Tangka of the primordial Buddha Samantabhadra, in union with consort. Chiwong Monstery, Nepal, 1996.*

Following pages: *Two lamas perform ritual prayers at a cremation ceremony. Humla, Nepal, 1985.*

The term bardo by itself simply means 'in between', in the sense of the gap or space between two experiences. When used in a general way it refers to the gap or space between death and rebirth. Thus phrases like 'bardo visions' and 'bardo path', which so often appear in Tibetan literature, refer to what is experienced during the period of a person's unfoldment after the moment of death and until the moment of rebirth.

Mention was made earlier of the two tantric systems that came to Tibet from India some three centuries prior to Karma Lingpa releasing his magnum opus, *The Tibetan Book of the Dead.* Called 'The Six Yogas of Naropa' and 'The Six Yogas of Niguma', both these systems speak of a link between the dream body and the bardo body. For this reason, the dream yogas are taught as a prerequisite to the bardo yogas in both systems.

Lama Tsongkhapa (1357-1419) makes an interesting statement in his commentary on the Six Yogas of Naropa, and says that in the early days the

Prayer flags adorn a high mountain pass, symbolizing the five elements of earth, water, fire, air and space. Bhutan, 2004.

Wisdom deity Vajrapani, Revealer of the Tantras, in sexual union with his consort. He holds the vajra *of enlightenment energy in his right hand and the bell of primordial emptiness wisdom in his left. She holds a slicing knife in her right, to cut off the head of duality-grasping, and in her left holds a human skull filled with the blood of blissful wisdom. Painting from the seventeenth or eighteenth century. Tibet, 1990. (© Libermann Collection)*

Facing page: *Tangka of Padma Sambhava, the Indian tantric master who taught in Tibet in the eighth century and was the founder of the Nyingma School of Tibetan Buddhism.*

Lama Tsongkhapa, a famous commentator on the Six Yogas tradition and the guru of the young First Dalai Lama, flanked by his two disciples. Dharamsala, India, 1970.

system was known as the *Bardo Trangdol gi Men Ngak*, or 'Oral Transmission for Achieving Liberation in the Bardo'. He states that this was generally the name used by Marpa and Milarepa, the first two generations of Tibetan masters in the lineage of transmission. It is clear that in this context the term bardo has a larger meaning than merely the after-death state.

Marpa also termed his system 'The Yoga of the Three Blendings', and this throws light on the expression 'The Oral Transmission for Achieving Liberation in the Bardo'. The three blendings refer to the daytime practice or kundalini yogas for inducing the death simulation process; the night-time practice, which refers to the yogas of sleep and dream; and finally the yogas of the blendings at the time of death.

Tsongkhapa goes on to say that success in the kundalini yogas and death simulation process during the daytime meditation sessions establishes the ability to succeed in the night-time yogas of sleep and dream, and that this in turn bestows the ability to succeed in the yogas to be applied at the time of death.

The Tibetan Book of the Dead unpacks these three bardo states and makes them into six. The bardo of death becomes threefold: the bardo of dying, which refers to the process of energy dissolutions leading up to the moment of death; the bardo of reality itself, which refers to the clear light experience at the moment of death; and the bardo of becoming, which refers to the unwinding process, with its alluring and terrifying bardo visions that occur after leaving the clear light. The remaining three (of the six) in this tradition have to do with rebirth, and with the daytime and night-time bardos during one's lifetime.

An understanding of Marpa's three blendings is relevant to an understanding of *The Tibetan Book of the Dead* on a number of levels, but primarily because it points out the nature of the three primary links between life and death. In Buddhism these links are known as the 'three kayas': *dharmakaya, sambhogakaya* and *nirmanakaya*. These refer to the three dimensions of a full enlightenment. In Sutrayana one works to achieve these three in the future with enlightenment; in the Vajrayana, to which the Six Yogas and the *Bardo Todol* traditions both belong, one instead looks for aspects of ordinary experience that are in synchronicity with each of the three, and establishes identification and a meditational link with those aspects. This is the key to the tantric process and to a successful practice of the Mandala of 100 Peaceful and Wrathful Deities. Moreover, it is the key to a successful reading of *The Tibetan Book of the Dead.*

The first of the three is the daytime blending. This yoga involves controlling the subtle body energies and invoking a near-death experience. The clear light consciousness is aroused, and experienced just as at the time of death. Sevenfold energy dissolution leads up to this invocation of clear light consciousness as is experienced at the time of death. The yogi blends this with the *dharmakaya* or the formless bliss aspect of the enlightenment experience, and remains immersed in it for as long as possible.

Eventually the subtle karmic winds begin to stir, and the energies that had been dissolved begin to manifest again. The meditator emerges from the formless clear light into a blissful realm of form with joyful feelings and thoughts. This is like emerging from the clear light at the time of death and assuming a bardo body. The yogi blends this with the blissful *sambhogakaya* aspect of enlightenment. If he has the ability, he then swims back upstream to the clear light again; if not, he continues with the blissful form experience for the remainder of the meditation session. Finally he arises from his meditation cushion and re-enters ordinary life. This is like rebirth, and the experience is blended with the *nirmanakaya* aspect of enlightenment.

The night-time experience involves controlling the energies at the time of going to sleep, and following their absorptions consciously. Eventually they all absorb just as at the time of death, and the clear light of the moment of sleep arises. The yogi blends this with the *dharmakaya* aspect of enlightenment, and remains there for as long as possible. Eventually the karmic winds stir, and the yogi exits the clear light. One by one the energies awaken and the sleeping yogi assumes a dream body. This is similar in nature to the bardo body, and the yogi blends the experience with the blissful *sambhogakaya.* If he can, he pushes the dream in reverse, and re-enters the clear light. If not, he pursues the dream yoga for as long as possible, blending the experience with the *sambhogakaya,* and taking all dream experiences as pure

A moment of transcendence, Sarnath Stupa, India.

mandala visions. Eventually he awakens from sleep and dream, and arises into waking consciousness. This is like rebirth, and the experience is blended with the *nirmanakaya* aspect of enlightenment.

The above two aspects of practice – daytime and night-time – can be practised on either of the two tantric levels: generation stage, which involves meditative concentration and visualization; and completion stage, which involves complete mastery of the chakra, *nadi* and prana practices. Obviously, the latter is superior.

Finally, the three blendings at the time of death is the nature of the instruction given in *The Tibetan Book of the Dead.* As the moment of death approaches, the yogi attempts to consciously follow the process of the dissolution of the elemental energies. When the clear light of death arises, he retains it firmly, and blends it with the *dharmakaya* instruction. If enlightenment is not attained at that time, the subtle energies begin to stir, and he emerges from the clear light into the after-death state, complete with a bardo body. He attempts to blend this with the *sambhogakaya,* and if successful, then to reverse the process toward the clear light of *dharmakaya.* When the yoga is properly applied, he achieves enlightenment in the clear light of death as experienced in the bardo. He then has complete control over the rebirth process, and can manifest a *nirmanakaya* aspect wherever in the universe he would be of greatest benefit to living beings.

The above discussion covers three of the four topics that are the focus of this chapter. As for the fourth topic – sex – here too, the Dvakpo Kargyu tradition of the Six Yogas of Naropa offer us an interesting perspective.

Sometimes the Six Yogas of Naropa are listed as ten. This is done by breaking some of the more detailed and elaborate of the six yogas into parts and listing these separately.

In particular the first of the six, known in Tibetan as *tummo* or 'inner fire', is easily broken up into segments. When this is done, one of the segments is called *karmamudra* in Sanskrit, or *ley gya* in Tibetan. The term literally translates as 'seal of destiny', and refers to a partner used in the tantric sexual yogas.

The 'Stupa of 100,000 Buddhas' in Gyantse, Tibet, 1990.

As the First Dalai Lama explains it in a commentary he wrote on the six *Kalachakra* yogas,[1] '*Karmamudra* is explained as the practice performed with a maiden possessing the physical attributes of a woman, such as beautiful hair and so forth, with whom one has a strong karmic link. Here the maiden herself has the ability to induce the full experience by means of her skilful embrace, without reliance on the powers of meditation.' He goes on to quote the eighth-century Sanskrit work known as the *Vimalaprabha*, or *Stainless Light*. This text states,

> *Karmamudra* is the maiden who gives the falling bliss . . . How is this so? If the yogi is unable to control the movement of the drops solely through the power of meditation, he takes up the practice of *karmamudra*. Because the *karmamudra* gives him the power to direct the vital substances to the tip of the jewel, she is called 'the maiden who bestows the falling bliss'. One sits in union . . . which causes the substances to melt and come to the tip of the jewel. Not only are these to be prevented from slipping; they must also be prevented from flowing into other sites.

In the Six Yogas of Naropa, *karmamudra* is tacked on to the end of *tummo*, or inner fire, the Tibetan equivalent of the kundalini yogas. The early stages of these yogas are accomplished by physical exercises, power breathing, and the chakra/prana/*bindhu* applications. For the final stage of *tummo*, however, the sexual yogas are required.

The theory behind the application is that the energy transformations leading up to the experience of sexual orgasm are very much like the energy dissolutions at the time of death. Moreover, at the time of sexual orgasm the clear light mind arises, just as at the time of death.

Thus for those unable to invoke and control the energy withdrawals and movements of the *bindhu* or subtle drops solely through the power of meditation, it is wise to look to the similarities of the clear light of sexual orgasm, the clear light invoked by the kundalini peak experience, the clear

The tantric deity Kalachakra and consort in sexual union. Bodh Gaya, India, 1990.

light of the moment of falling asleep, and the clear light of the moment of death.

Khyungpo Naljor, who brought the Six Yogas of Niguma to Tibet, wrote a text called *Instruction on the Three Bardo States*, or *Bardo Sum gi Men Ngak*. The meaning of the term 'bardo' in this context is much the same as in the Six Yogas of Naropa from the Marpa tradition as discussed above. However, the Niguma Yogas place a greater emphasis upon the sexual yogas. Here the three bardos of waking state, sleep and dream, and after-death experience are the topics of investigation. The clear light of the waking state primarily refers to the clear light invoked through the peak *tummo* experience while engaged in the sexual yogas.

The discussion is very much relevant to a reading of *The Tibetan Book of the Dead*. Familiarizing oneself with these yogic applications while alive brings about the ability to recognize and sustain the clear light experience at the moment of death, and to work effectively with the bardo yogas in the after-death state.

This is clearly stated by Lama Tsongkhapa in his commentary on the Naropa Yogas, where he unequivocally writes,

> The greater the success with the yogas in the waking state, the greater will be one's success with the yogas of sleep and dream. Then by extension the greater one's success with the clear light of sleep and the application of the dream yogas, the greater will be one's success with the yogas to be applied when the death experience arrives, the clear light of death is made manifest, and one enters into the bardo of after-death with its many alluring and terrifying appearances.

It should be noted that the bardo yogas are not limited to the *anuttara*-yoga-tantras, although they are more sophisticated in these high systems. We find them even in the *kriya* class.

For example, in a verse work intended as a teaching manual that the Third Dalai Lama wrote on the Indian *mahasiddha* Tsimbupa's lineages of Avalokiteshvara practice, the Third speaks of the tradition as having seven levels of training. The last of the seven is termed 'The Yoga for Achieving Enlightenment in the Bardo'. The Third writes,

> Lastly, here is the method for practising
> The yoga for gaining enlightenment
> In the bardo, or the state
> Between death and rebirth.
>
> Like a flash of lightning in a cloud
> And like a fish rising from the depths of a pond,
> The clear light of death manifests
> And subtle consciousness and energy
> Enter into the bardo state.
>
> Transform the body into the divine nature
> Of a tantric deity and mystic mandala;
> Transform speech into the mandala of mantras;
> Transform the mind itself into awareness
> Of the transcendental nature of suchness.
> Remain inseparable from these three mandalas.
>
> In this way you can control your own destiny,
> Consciously directing your mind to a rebirth
> In a pure realm, or as a human or celestial being,
> And can thus achieve once more a physical form
> Most appropriate to dwelling in the ways of dharma.
> This is the nature of the yogic technique
> To be applied in the bardo
> For the sake of achieving
> Higher rebirth and enlightenment.

Following pages: *Wall fresco of the wrathful* herukas, *in sexual union with their consorts. Pharping, Nepal, 2007.*

Chapter Seven

Bypassing the Bardo, Purification in the Bardo and Caring for the Dead

A variant form of Vajrakilaya, the wrathful meditation deity that brings instant release from all obstacles. This is the main mantra/mandala practice that is cultivated today by most lamas who maintain the tradition of the Bardo Todol. *Tashi Jong, India, 1990.*

The *Bardo Todol* is part of a larger Tibetan tradition known as *Bardo Jang Chok* or 'Ritual for Purification in the Bardo'. Every school of Tibetan Buddhism has its own ritual manuals that it uses for this. The *Bardo Todol* is unique in that it utilizes the Mandala of 100 Peaceful and Wrathful Deities. Otherwise the process of bardo purification is much the same. The *Bardo Todol* is also unique in the depth that it brings to the section known as *Bardo Ngo Tro* or 'Pointing Out the Nature of the Bardo'. Buddhists believe that most people who have passed away wander without recognizing their state, and that the first step in successful navigation of the dangerous bardo waters is a realization that one is dead. For this reason Karma Lingpa's text continually calls out to the deceased to look at the experience and recognize it for what it is.

The opening section of the text mentions *powa* or 'transference'. It states that the deceased's lama should perform *powa* on the person, for if it succeeds

Powa *ceremony for directly transferring consciousness to a buddha-field or a higher rebirth, and thus bypassing the bardo experience altogether. Drigung, Tibet, 1990.*

there will be no bardo experience and consequently no need for a reading of the *Bardo Todol*. *Powa* refers to the practice of forcefully throwing a person's consciousness into a pure rebirth.

As a personal practice *powa* is listed as one of the Six Yogas of Naropa and Six Yogas of Niguma. When applied in this way the yogi 'opens' the death channel by means of meditation. This is done when the practitioner is still young and healthy. Once this death channel has been opened, the yogi can easily apply *powa* when the time of death arrives. Tibetans call the tradition *Ma Gom Sangyey*, or 'Enlightenment without Meditation', because the simple practice brings about certain rebirth in a pure land, where enlightenment is easily achieved. Most tantric systems have their own methods of *powa*.

If the dying person has not mastered the *powa* technique and cleared the death channel of the body while still alive, it is possible for a lama or even a friend who is an advanced practitioner to assist with the process at the time of death. Performing *powa* for disciples is a common activity among high lamas, and is something the personal guru of the deceased is usually requested to do.

In a verse, the Seventh Dalai Lama writes how the many occasions on which he is asked to do *powa* for disciples serve to remind him of his own approaching death,

> They die young, they die old, day after day.
> I am asked to perform *powa* for them,
> Or to prophesy their conditions of rebirth.
> My mind turns to thoughts of my own death.

Karma Lingpa also mentions that the dying person or his assisting ritualist should observe signs of death and rebirth. Another Treasure Text (*see* next chapter) in Karma Lingpa's *Collected Works* explains just how this is done.[1] The idea is that these signs will provide clues of whether *powa* should be applied or a guided reading of the *Bardo Todol* would be more appropriate.

A number of other Tibetan Buddhist attitudes towards the care of the dying and dead emerge from the *Bardo Todol*. One is that relatives who are crying or wailing should keep a discreet distance from the body. The belief is that the body acts as a magnet to the wandering spirit in the days after a person's death, and the sight of people in grief and despair can be distracting and harmful. Of course people are always deeply saddened by the loss of a loved one, but the expression of this grief should be sublimated by concern for the well-being of the deceased. Rather than being overwhelmed by the loss, people should offer prayers and good wishes to assist the deceased in his journey.

Those who have trained well and made good progress, but who have not accomplished enlightenment before dying, are directed to do so while wandering in the bardo. If they still fail, they should strive diligently to achieve an auspicious rebirth to continue towards enlightenment in the next life.

Karma Lingpa here mentions a doctrinal point made by Buddha in the *abhidharma* literature. When those who fail to achieve enlightenment in the bardo have exhausted their wandering karma and the time for rebirth draws near, they see visions of couples making love. Eventually the vision of one of the couples will dominate attention, and those of other lovers disappear. The wandering soul then develops a deep sexual attraction for the person of the opposite gender of the one he or she is to take, and a deep anger toward the person of the same gender. This anger causes the death of the bardo body, and the wandering soul plunges into the seminal fluids like a shooting star. Thus sexual attraction to the mother signals rebirth as a male, and sexual attraction to the father signals rebirth as a female, with a concordant anger toward the person of the same sex. Much has been made of this Buddhist equivalent of the Oedipus complex in Western writing. Karma Lingpa expresses it with eloquence and simplicity.

Buddhists also believe that the soul often stays in the body for a number of days after the outer signs of death are manifest, and so usually try not to have an unqualified person disturb it in any way for at least three days. A qualified person is someone well versed in reading the signs and omens of the death and transmigration process, and in performing *powa* or other death-related rituals and methods.

It is important to mention that death rituals such as the *Bardo Todol* not only benefit the dead, but also the living. Karma Lingpa points out several

times that the attitudes of the people deeply grieved by the loss of a loved one can have a strong effect on the evolution of the wandering soul of the deceased. He goes on to say that offering prayers and good wishes, rather than expressing the anguish of personal loss, is the appropriate response.

Readers well versed in Tibetan Buddhism will know that the first five days of the bardo visions involve the appearances of the buddhas of the five families: Vairochana, Akshobya, Ratnasambhava, Amitabha and Amoghasiddhi. All *anuttara*-yoga-tantra mandalas are divided into five principal sections: the four cardinal directions and the centre. The five buddhas are each connected to one of the five sections.

These five buddhas are common to all *anuttara*-yoga-tantra systems, although each system has its own manner of arranging them in its mandala. In general, the five buddhas symbolize the transformation of the five

Above: *Buddhist stupas, repositories for sacred objects and for the remains of the funeral pyres of high beings. Til, Limi, Nepal, 2000.*

skandhas or aspects of a person into the five enlightenment qualities. That is to say, when we achieve enlightenment our five individual *skandhas* become these five buddhas.

Each buddha is also associated with a basic element – earth, water, fire, air or space – and with a basic colour: yellow, white, red, green or blue. These are linked to the five root delusions or poisons: ignorance, attachment, anger, pride and jealousy. These five delusions are the principal causes of human suffering and the creator of all negative karma.

However, each of the five delusions has a wisdom aspect as well: infinity or *dharmadhatu*; mirror-like radiance; the wisdom of the equal preciousness of all things; distinguishing awareness or appreciation of the uniqueness of all things; and the wisdom that is able to accomplish all things effortlessly and spontaneously.

In brief, it can be said that the enlightenment experience consists of transforming the five delusions into the five wisdoms, and the five *skandhas* into the five buddhas. Thus the symbolism of these first five days of the bardo experience as described in the *Bardo Todol* are very much part of the general tantric picture.

Tantric initiates will also recognize these five transformative processes from the first of the four levels of the tantric initiation ceremony: vase, secret, wisdom and sacred word. In the vase initiation each of the five *skandhas* is isolated and transformed into one of the five buddhas, and each of the five delusions is activated, and the radiance of its primordial wisdom aspect is pointed out. In this way, through the five vase initiations the five *skandhas* become the five buddhas and the five delusions become the five wisdoms.

Because of this aspect of the initiation ritual and the similarity of this phase to the *Bardo Todol,* advanced practitioners often perform self-initiation on the day of their passing. If they are too weak to do so personally, they will invite a teacher or senior dharma brother to perform it in the same room on their behalf, so they can meditate on the stages and listen to the unfolding process.

Facing page: *The retinue of* herukas, *or wrathful deities, symbolic of the aggressive nature of the mind transformed into expressions of enlightenment. Painting from the seventeenth or eighteenth century. Tibet, 1990. (© Zimmerman Family Collection)*

Following pages: *At a sky burial, vultures wait patiently for the feast while it is prepared as the last act of charity and generosity on behalf of the deceased. Drigung, Tibet, 1990.*

Chapter Eight

Karma Lingpa, the Bardo Todol and the Treasure Text Tradition

Dorje Trolo, a wrathful form of Padma Sambhava, who inspired the visions that served as the source of Karma Lingpa's Bardo Todol. *Tibet, 1977.*

Karma Lingpa, the lama who originally brought out *The Tibetan Book of the Dead* in fourteenth-century Tibet, was born in the Dvakpo, the stronghold of the Marpa tradition of the Six Yogas. In fact Marpa's lineages are often referred to as the Dvakpo Kargyu School, because the first monastery of the school descending from Marpa was built by Milarepa's disciple Gampopa in Dvakpo. Therefore, Karma Lingpa was well versed in the yogic legacy of 'the three blendings on three occasions', particularly in the bardo doctrines from Marpa.

Moreover, Karma Lingpa was born into a family with strong links to the Dvakpo Kargyu. The first part of his name, 'Karma', suggests that his family was affiliated with the Karma Kargyu, one of the four older sub-sects of the Dvakpo Kargyu. Even today, members of this Kargyu sub-sect traditionally receive 'Karma' as a prefix to their names.

However, Karma Lingpa is not credited with the authorship of *The Tibetan Book of the Dead.* The text is attributed to the eighth-century subcontinental master Padma Sambhava. It is generally believed that Padma Sambhava spoke the words and his female disciple Yeshey Tsogyal transcribed them. However, this is something of an honorific manner of speaking. The text is part of a larger Tibetan tradition known as *Terma*, or 'Treasure', which is found in both the Nyingma and Bon schools of Tibetan Buddhism, and uses the same name in both. *The Tibetan Book of the Dead* is part of the illustrious legacy of the former.

Traditional scriptures state that the world in general and Tibet in particular were not ready for the full range of Padma Sambhava's teachings at the time he travelled and taught in Central Asia. Consequently, he wrote many texts and hid them in sacred places, sealing and protecting them through mystical powers, with the aim of having them discovered and revealed to future generations when the times were sufficiently mature to receive them. The beings destined to reveal and propagate these Treasures were designated as *Ter Ton*, or 'Treasure Revealers'.

Karma Lingpa is one of the most famous of the early Treasure Revealers, and his *Bardo Todol* is the most famous of the many Treasures he revealed. His *Collected Works* lists over a dozen of these Treasures.

It is generally said that these Treasures are of four main kinds: *Beyter* or 'Hidden Treasures', *Gong Ter* or 'Meditational Treasures', *Milam Terma* or 'Dream Treasures', and *Daknang Terma*, or 'Pure Vision Treasures'.

Some lamas believe that the *Beyter* or Hidden Treasures were physically concealed by Padma Sambhava and Yeshey Tsogyal, and later brought out of their repositories. However, other lamas speak of a more mystical process. They say that Padma Sambhava 'buried' the Treasures in the mindstreams of several of his twenty-five chief disciples, and instructed them to be reborn in future centuries, when the teachings would be relevant.

This legacy is attached to the mythology surrounding Karma Lingpa, for he is said to have been a reincarnation or emanation of one of this group of twenty-five inner sanctum mystics. Karma Lingpa took rebirth in Dvakpo some 500 years after Padma Sambhava's appearance in Tibet, and as a youth went about his life in an ordinary manner. One day, he passed a sacred site on Gampo Ri that had been consecrated by Padma Sambhava

Following pages: *A line of stupas decorated with rocks, with mantric syllables carved into them. Most sacred sites in Tibet have resident carvers who prepare rocks in this way at the request of pilgrims. Tibet, 2005.*

and Yeshey Tsogyal, and the Treasures buried inside his mindstream were activated. He then proceeded to transcribe them.

Because of the mystical manner in which the Treasures are hidden and revealed, something of the Revealer's nature seeps into them, as well as his time and place. His particular background, character and education inform and give a contemporary character to the Treasure.

Thus Karma Lingpa's background in the Karma Kargyu and the various traditions of the Six Yogas brings a particular flavour to the manner in which the Treasure is expressed. Gampo Ri, the place where the cycle of texts was revealed to Karma Lingpa, is the name of the mountain on which Milarepa's chief disciple Gampopa built the first Dvakpo Kargyu monastery. This is another indication of the *Bardo Todol's* link with the Six Yogas tradition from Marpa and Milarepa.

Above: *The Dirapuk side (north face) of Mount Kailash on the outer* khorra. *Tibet, 2005.*

Facing page: *Thirteen stupas on the pass dividing the eastern and western segments of the inner* khorra *to Mt Kailash, 19,020 feet above sea level. Tibet, 2005.*

Following pages: Mountain settlement with prayer flags. Ringmo, Dolpo, Nepal, 2003.

The way that a Treasure revelation is given a contemporary context is perhaps best illustrated by a Treasure revealed in the mid-1940s to a Nyingma lama called Khamtrul Yeshey Dorje. While taking a break from his meditations one day, he saw an airplane 'flying the hump', an Air Force expression for the American planes that flew supplies from India to China to support Chinese resistance to the Japanese occupation. The lama had never seen an airplane before, and was amazed at its shape and sound. He knew of cars and trains, of course, from the stories of the many Tibetans who had gone on pilgrimage to British India, and had probably even seen photographs of them.

The night after seeing his first plane he dreamed of Padma Sambhava and Yeshey Tsogyal. Padma Sambhava looked at him and said,

When iron birds fly
And horses run on wheels,
My dharma will travel
To the land of the Red Man.[1]

The next day Khamtrul Yeshey Dorje wrote out his dream sequence and the words of prophecy. The verse was catchy, and travelled by word of mouth through the general lama grapevine. Soon it was well known to most lamas in his circle of teachers, friends and disciples. The Dalai Lama quoted it in a public lecture he gave to a group of lamas during his visit to India in 1956.

After the Tibetans came to India and saw both trains and planes, and also read about the North American native Indians, they remembered this verse of prophecy. They also soon learned of the American legacy of anti-

Above: *Monks visiting a mountain shrine in Zhang Zhung, Tibet, 2005.*

Following pages: *Stupa on Mount Kailash, western side circumambulation. Tibet, 2005.*

Communism, and since their country had been lost to Communist China they felt an instant rapport with the US.

From that time on every Tibetan lama wanted to teach in America, the Land of the Red Man, and play a role in fulfilling Padma Sambhava's dream words to Khamtrul Yeshey Dorje.

Since then the verse has been quoted in a dozen Buddhist books and countless Buddhist magazine articles. It is usually presented as words actually written by Padma Sambhava in the mid-eighth century. That it was actually formulated and expressed in the dreams of a sleeping Tibetan lama in the 1940s after he saw his first airplane is rarely given a footnote.

The *Terma* tradition would say that the passing airplane was merely an external condition activating the Treasure prophecy that had been buried in Khamtrul Yeshey Dorje's mindstream in a previous life. Of course the expression of the prophecy – the form it took – was tailored to suit the conditions of the time, just as wine poured into a vessel assumes the shape of that vessel.

Today there are an estimated 1,000 centres of various sizes and shapes in the United States for the study and practice of Tibetan Buddhism, which is a partial fulfilment of the prophecy.

This idea of Treasure Teachings being buried in the mindstreams of particular trainees to be activated and re-expressed centuries later has proved to be one of the most rich and dynamic forces in Tibetan Buddhism, allowing for a continual revision and transformation of the living tradition. It has its precedence in Classical Buddhist India, where most Mahayana sutras are not spoken by Buddha himself but by his chief disciples, such as Avalokiteshvara and Manjushri. Similarly, although the Buddhist tantras are attributed to Buddha, very few of them are spoken directly by him.

Padma Sambhava has remained the mythological source for all the thousands of Treasures that have been revealed over the centuries. Again, this has had a powerful impact on the tradition. Attaching his name to each Treasure ensures that the tradition will retain a sanctity and commitment to excellence that would otherwise be difficult to maintain, just as attaching Buddha's name to all the Mahayana sutras and Vajrayana tantras has done the same for them.

Part Two

A Condensed Translation of the Bardo Todol or The Tibetan Book of the Dead

Offering of light at Sarnath Stupa as part of Kalachakra teaching. India, 2005.

From the Self-Liberation Cycle of the Profound Dharma
of the Mandala of Peaceful and Wrathful Deities,
Here is the Book for Recitation known as
The Great Book for Liberation by Hearing in the Bardo

A tangka painting of Amitabha, the Buddha of Boundless Light. Here, Amitabha symbolizes the deathless aspect of enlightenment and the timeless radiance of the universal mind.

Karma Lingpa's Preface

Buddha Amitabha, who is *dharmakaya*;
The peaceful and wrathful lotus deities, who are *sambhogakaya*;
And Padma Sambhava, *nirmanakaya* protector of living beings:
Homage to the lama as these three kayas.

This method for mediocre yogis to gain liberation in the bardo,
The great text for achieving liberation through hearing,
Is presented in three sections:
The foreword; the actual text; and the afterword.

As for the first of these, the foreword, here it is said
That those of superior capacity – the great yogis –
 should gain liberation
During this very lifetime by relying on the stages of practice.
If they do not succeed in this, then they should apply
The methods of consciousness at the time of death.

Padma Sambhava, to whom Karma Lingpa dedicates the opening verse of The Tibetan Book of the Dead, *sits in sexual union with Yeshey Tsogyal, a Tibetan princess who became both his lover and also his chief disciple. They are surrounded by male and female deities in sexual union. Painting from early nineteenth century. Tibet, 1997.*

Even mediocre yogis can gain liberation in this way.
However, if they do not succeed in the effort,
Then they should turn to a reading of this text,
For achieving liberation through hearing in the bardo.

If the yogi wants to attempt this consciousness transference, he[1] should observe the onsetting signs of the death process, and look at them as clearly as watching them manifest in a mirror. Then when the signs of the final stage of death have arisen, he should recollect and apply the *powa* method of release. If this transference method is successful, then there is no need for a reading of this *Bardol Todol* text.

However, if the *powa* technique does not work, then the ritualist should sit near the body and clearly chant this *Bardo Todol.*

In cases where the body is not present, then the ritualist should sit on the dead person's meditation seat or bed, and should summon forth the soul of the person (from wherever it might be wandering) by means of pronouncing the words of truth, visualizing that it comes into the room and listens to the reading. When this has been done the reading of the *Bardo Todol* can commence.

It is not appropriate for the sounds of the cries and laments of relatives and friends to be present during this phase of the ceremony, so loved ones who are overwhelmed with grief should not be allowed to participate.

If the reading is being performed in the presence of the dying person, then it should commence as soon as the outer breath has ceased. It is best if it is done by the person's lama, *vajra* brother, or close friend, but if these are not available then anyone who has achieved spiritual clarity and had a harmonious relationship with the deceased can perform it.

Similarly, there is no need to perform a reading for a person who can apply *powa* or consciousness transference to a pure realm at the time of death, or if a lama can successfully perform this for him. When *powa* is properly done the person immediately takes rebirth in a pure realm, and completely bypasses the bardo.[2]

Cremation of His Eminence Chogye Trichen Rinpoche. Boudhnath, Kathmandu, 2008.

A Preliminary to the Actual Reading

The ritualist should begin by arranging an elaborate altar with extensive offerings for the buddhas and bodhisattvas, and then chanting the offering rite three times. The offerings can be arranged physically, or if this is not possible then they can simply be visualized and mentally emanated.

He should tunefully chant a prayer to the buddhas and bodhisattvas, requesting blessings for their assistance. This should be done three or seven times close to the ear of the deceased.

After that he should chant a prayer for protection from the dangers of the bardo, a prayer for achieving liberation in the bardo, and the basic bardo verses.

The actual *Bardo Todol* should then be read three or seven times.

•

Translator's comments: The prayer liturgies listed above are all found in Karma Lingpa's *Collected Works*. However, they are rarely used. Instead, lamas of all schools of Tibetan Buddhism tend to replace them with the *Zangcho Monlam* or *Prayer of Sublime Ways*.

This text is also known as *The Prayer of Samantabhadra,* because it is the essence of the *Avatamsaka Sutra,* and was pronounced by the Bodhisattva Samantabhadra. Nyingma lamas love it because of the Samantabhadra connection. Everyone else loves it for its function of serving as the essence of the *Avatamsaka.* Almost all Tibetan monks and lamas know it by heart.

I attach my translation of it below, because it is the most commonly used of all prayer liturgies that are read at the time of a death. It is usually chanted three or seven times as a preliminary to chanting *The Tibetan Book of*

Above: *Samantabhadra and Samantabhadri in sexual union, the all-perfect primordial buddhas. Their nakedness symbolizes the unconstructed and formless nature of* dharmakaya *wisdom. Detail from tangka on page 169.*

the Dead. In general the text is written as a dedication spoken by Bodhisattva Samantabhadra, and is presented in the first person (I, me, my, mine, etc.). However, when read for a deceased person this case is only retained in the opening verses that comprise the seven-limbed worship: prostration, making offerings, acknowledging personal faults, rejoicing in goodness, asking the buddhas to turn the wheel of dharma, asking them to remain forever, and the dedication of merits. After this, in the main body of the liturgy, the famous 'I' becomes 'he', or 'you', etc., because it is spoken for or to the deceased.

•

O lions amongst men,
Buddhas past, present, and future,
To as many of you as exist in the ten directions
I bow with body, speech, and mind.

On waves of strength of this king
Of prayers for exalted sublime ways,
With bodies as numerous as atoms of the world
I bow to the buddhas pervading space.

On every atom is found a buddha
Sitting amongst countless buddha sons,
I look with eyes of faith to the victorious ones
Thus filling the entire *dharmadhatu.*

Of these with endless oceans of excellence
Endowed with an ocean of wondrous speech
I sing praises of the greatness of all buddhas,
A eulogy to those gone to bliss.

Garlands of flowers I offer them,
And beautiful sounds, supreme perfumes,
Butter lamps and sacred incense,
I offer to all the victorious ones.

Excellent food, supreme fragrances,
And a mound of mystic substances high as Mount Meru
I arrange in a special formation
And offer to those who have conquered themselves.

And all peerless offerings I hold up
In admiration of those gone to bliss;
With the strength of faith in sublime ways
I bow and make offerings to the conquerors.

Long overpowered by attachment, aversion, and ignorance
We have collected much negative karma
With acts of body, speech, and mind.
Each and every one of these I now acknowledge.

In the perfections of the buddhas and bodhisattvas,
The *arhats,* training and beyond,
And in the latent goodness of every living being,
I lift up my heart and rejoice.

O lights into the ten directions,
Buddhas who have found the passionless stage of enlightenment,
To all of you I direct this request:
Turn the incomparable wheel of dharma.

O masters wishing to show *parinirvana,*
I beseech you to stay with us and teach,
For as many eons as there are specks of dust,
In order to bring goodness and joy to all beings.

May any small merits that we have amassed
By thus prostrating, making offerings, confessing, rejoicing,
And asking the buddhas to remain and teach the dharma,
Be dedicated now to supreme and perfect enlightenment.

May our offerings be received by all past buddhas
And by all those now abiding in the ten directions,
And may all the buddhas who have not yet come
Quickly perfect their minds and attain full awakening.

May all the buddha-realms of the ten directions
Remain forever vast and completely pure,
May the world be completely filled with buddhas who have attained
illumination under sacred trees,
And may they all be surrounded by bodhisattvas.

May all living beings in the ten directions
Always abide in health and joy.
May they live in accord with the way of dharma
And may their every wish be fulfilled.

By observing the ways of enlightenment
May the deceased remember his past lives in all reincarnations,
And in all cycles of death, migration, and rebirth
May a sensitivity for truth be ever strong in him.

By following in the footsteps of the buddhas
May he utterly perfect the sublime ways of the bodhisattvas,
And may he practise the faultless, undegenerating, stainless,
And pure ways of self-control.

In future lives may the deceased master all languages
That exist, including those of
The gods, *yakshas,* spirits, and varieties of men,
As well as all forms of communication of living beings,
That he may be able to show truth in every way.

Striving thus and in the transcending perfections
May he never forget the enlightenment mind,
And may he totally cleanse from within his mindstream
All negativities and mental veils.

May he gain freedom from karma, delusion, and karmic *maras*[1]
To be able to live in the world unaffected by its stains
Like an unstained lotus grows in the mud,
And like the sun and moon shine without obstruction in the sky.

For as long as there are buddha-fields and directions
May he strive to quell the misery of the lower realms,
May he bring only happiness to others
And place them all in goodness and joy.

May he strive to complete the ways of enlightenment
And to abide in ways harmonious with the world;
May he expose to others the ways most sublime
And himself abide in them throughout all future eons.

May his ways and the ways of a bodhisattva
Always go together hand in hand.
In body, speech, and mind
May he attune to their sublime ways.

May he never be separated from the good friends
Who reveal the path of the sublime ways
And who wish only to benefit him;
May he never disappoint them for even a moment.

May he constantly envision the perfect buddhas,
The protectors who are surrounded by bodhisattvas,
And in the future may he never weary
Of devoting himself to them with all his strength.

May he forever uphold the ways of enlightenment
And illumine the sublime way of truth;
May he practise throughout all future ages
The ways of deeds of the sublime path.

Wherever he goes in the various realms of existence
May he amass inexhaustible goodness and wisdom;
And may he become an unending treasure of qualities
Such as methods, wisdom, samadhi, and the experience of a bodhisattva.

In every atom are buddha-fields numberless as atoms,
Each field is filled with buddhas beyond conception,
And each buddha is surrounded by myriad bodhisattvas:
To all these dwellers in sublime ways we turn our attention.

Thus, in all atoms within the directions
Abide within the space of a single hair
An ocean of buddhas within an ocean of buddha-fields
Performing enlightened activities for an ocean of eons.

Each buddha with his perfect speech releases
An ocean of sounds with every word he says
To satisfy the infinitely diverse tendencies of beings:
Thus does the speech of a buddha constantly flow.

All these conquerors past, present, and future
Continually turn the methods of dharma wheels;
With all the powers of our mind we listen
For the inexhaustible sound of their words.

All future eons that could possibly be
Manifest within us in a single instant;
And we in a fraction of a moment
Enter into all these eons of the three times.

All past, present, and future lions among men
We envision with the instantaneous wisdom
And by the power of the bodhisattvas' examples
We focus upon the objects of their experience.

We manifest buddha-fields past, present, and future
Upon one single atom of existence,
And then we transform every single atom
Of existence into a buddha-field.

O deceased one, when the future lights of the worlds
Eventually gain enlightenment, turn their dharma wheels,
And reveal the passing to nirvana's supreme peace,
May you take rebirth in their very presence.

Then may you attain the ten powers:
The power of instant magical emanation,
The power that is a vehicle with every door,
The power of excellent activity,
The power of all-pervading love,
The power of constantly positive energy,
The power of passionless wisdom,
The powers of knowledge, method, and samadhi,
And the power of enlightenment itself.

May you purify the power of karma,
May you crush the powers of delusion,
May you render powerless the powerful *maras,*
And may you perfect the powers of sublime ways.

May you purify an ocean of realms,
May you liberate an ocean of sentient beings,
May you see an ocean of truths,
And may you realize an ocean of wisdom.

May you perform an ocean of perfect deeds,
May you perfect an ocean of prayers,
May you revere an ocean of buddhas,
And may you practise untiringly for an ocean of eons.

Through our practice of the sublime bodhisattva ways
May we gain the enlightenment of buddhahood
And then fulfill the enlightened and sublime aspiration
Of the buddhas past, present, and future.

In order to match the ways of the sage
Called Samantabhadra, the always-sublime one,
Chief amongst the awakened ones' sons,
We now dedicate all virtues that we possess.

Just as the sublime sage Samantabhadra
Dedicated all pure practices of body, speech, and mind
To the attainment of a pure state and pure realms,
So do we now dedicate the fruit of all our efforts.

In order to engage in all sublime virtues
We offer the prayer of Manjushri;
In the future may we never become faint
In striving to perfect the exalted bodhisattvas' way.

May our deeds never reach a limit,
May our qualities of excellence become boundless,
And by abiding in immeasurable activity
May we find buddhahood, the state of limitless manifestation.

Limitless is the extent of space,
Limitless is the number of sentient beings,
And limitless is the karma and delusions of beings,
Such are the limits of our aspirations.

One may offer supreme ornaments of the buddha-fields
Of the ten directions to the conquerors,
And also offer the highest joys of men and gods
For eons numerous as atoms of the world.

But to read or hear *The King of Prayers*
With eyes looking toward supreme illumination
And faith shining in one's heart for even an instant
Gives birth to a far more superior merit.

Should anyone recite this aspiration of sublime ways
They will pass beyond all states of sorrow,
Rise above all inferior beings, and gain
A vision of Amitabha, Buddha of Infinite Light.

Even in this very lifetime
All sublime joys will be theirs;
The experiences of the all-sublime Samantabhadra,
Without obstructions, will quickly be theirs.

Merely by giving voice to these aspirations
Of the sublime ways of a bodhisattva,
The effects can only be known by an omniscient buddha.
Therefore, doubt not that it leads to enlightenment.

In order to follow the excellent examples set
By the wisdom of the bodhisattva Manjushri
And the always-sublime Samantabhadra,
All virtues we dedicate to their peerless ideals.

All conquerors passed into the three times
Have praised as supreme this peerless dedication.
Therefore we also dedicate all of our merits
To the sublime goals of a bodhisattva.

Now the moment of death has arrived.
May you remain free from the spiritual obscurations,
Perceive the face of Amitabha
And take birth in Sukhavati, the pure land of joy.

Having arrived there, may you fulfill
All aims of this prayer of aspirations
And benefit the countless living beings
Residing throughout the ten directions.

In the joyous mandala of Amitabha Buddha
May you dwell within a beautiful lotus,
And may you have the pleasure of gaining
A pure prophecy from Amitabha himself.

Having won this word of prophecy,
By the power of mind may you fill all directions
With many millions of mystical emanations
And bring limitless benefits to the world.

If by reciting this prayer of sublime ways
A tiny fragment of good karma arises,
May it work immediately to fulfill
All *dharmic* hopes of living beings.

This is followed by the actual *Bardo Todol* reading, which is in three sections: pointing out the clear light of the bardo of death; pointing out the nature of experience during the bardo of essential being; and pointing out the method of closing the gateway to the womb during the bardo of becoming.[2]

Mantra-carved mani *stones with animal horns create the impressive Mani wall running through Tirthapuri. The same red ochre is found on the ancient Zhang Zhung burial monuments and is often used to placate the* tsen *spirits of the middle realm.*

Pointing Out the Clear Light of the Bardo of Death

There are some practitioners who gained a good understanding during their lifetime but did not accomplish deep realization. Others might have achieved glimpses of insight but remained weak in terms of integration. Still others might be on ordinary levels, having neither received much instruction nor accomplished much practice. Nonetheless, some from amongst them will be able to recognize the primordial clear light mind that is the basis of all experience when this *Bardo Todol* teaching is applied at the time of dying, and will instantly attain the undying *dharmakaya* body at that time. They achieve enlightenment then and there, and will not have to enter the bardo.

The best is to have the instruction read by a root teacher from whom one received instruction. If he is not present, then a spiritual brother with whom one shares *samaya* is good. If even this is not possible, the instruction can be read by any spiritual friend. Should none of the above be present, anyone in the same lineage will suffice.

The late Dilgo Khyentsey Rinpoche, great lineage holder of The Tibetan Book of the Dead *tradition, teaches a group of monks at Shechen Monastery. Boudhnath, Nepal, 1988.*

The reading should be done with clear enunciation, and will have the effect of reminding the dying person of the nature of the instructions that had previously been received.

The time to apply the method is when the outer breath ceases. The subtle energies are dissolved into the central channel *avadhuti*, also known as the wisdom channel, and the unfabricated clear light consciousness arises with strength.

Otherwise, if the energies do not enter the central channel at this time but instead drain into the side channels, then the clear light experience will be very brief and the bardo visions will almost instantly begin to appear. Thus the method of avoiding this should be applied.

Generally the energy will remain in the central channel for approximately the length of time it takes to eat a meal. The effort should be made during that period.

If the person has the ability to effect the transference of consciousness just when the breath stops, this is best. If there is no confidence that this can be done, then the ritualist should begin reading the instruction when signs of imminent death arise, reciting repeatedly as follows into the ear of the dying person:

> O child of noble character, whose name is Such-and-Such, the time has come to choose a path. The breath has ceased, and the clear light of death is about to become manifest. This is known as the first bardo, the clear light experience.
>
> Previously your teacher had induced a clear light mind experience within you. Recollect this clear light mind now: empty like space, the final void nature of all things, radiant emptiness without inner centre or outer boundary. When this clear light consciousness arises, recognize and retain it, and rest within that sphere. Listen as I read this pointing-out to you.

Then when the breath stops the ritualist should move the position of the body into the Lion Posture, placing it on its right side with the right ring finger pressed against the right nostril, just as is done in the training in the yogas of sleep and dream. Simultaneously he should press on the two energy pathway points associated with sleep. This will encourage the subtle energies to remain in the central channel *avadhuti,* and will also encourage the consciousness to eventually leave the body by the crown aperture.

Now the actual reminder is given, for this is the time that all beings experience the first bardo, called 'the *dharmata* of clear light', and also 'the irreversible experience of *dharmakaya* mind'.

At the time when the outer breath has ceased but the inner energies are still in motion, the subtle energies begin to dissolve into the central channel. Untrained people can lose awareness of the process at this time.

How long this state (of clear light *dharmakaya* mind) will continue in a given individual will vary in dependence upon conditions such as the positive or negative quality of the vessel, the pace at which the energy dissolutions occurred, the level of tantric training the person achieved during his or her lifetime, the quality of the person's *shamata* power (meditative concentration), and the condition of the subtle energy pathways.

During this period the pointing-out should be repeatedly read. The sign (that the clear light experience has ended and consciousness has left the body) is that a drop of yellowish liquid will be released from the aperture of the sexual organ.

In general it is said that this clear light mind manifests for only a few fingersnaps of time in someone who is pressed by strongly negative karma, whereas it can continue for a very long time in more highly evolved people.

Most sutra and tantra scriptures suggest that it (i.e. consciousness remaining in the body) can continue for four-and-a-half days, and therefore they recommend that the deceased not be disturbed for this amount of time. The effort to point out the nature of the clear light experience should be maintained for that period.

It is useful to begin the application from the early signs of the imminent onset of death, when the death dissolution process has commenced.

Naturally it is best if the dying person is able to apply the yoga himself, without any assistance. However, if this cannot be done then a guru, a *vajra* brother, or someone with whom the deceased had a close spiritual relationship, should sit to the side, observe the signs of the dissolution of the subtle elemental energies, and point them out, saying,

> Pay attention. It seems that now the earth energies are dissolving into the water energies. You are losing the ability to move your limbs. Observe the inner signs.

And then:

> Now the water energies are dissolving into the fire energies. Your heartbeat is growing faint. Observe the inner signs.
>
> Now the fire energies are dissolving into the air energies. Your bodily temperature is dropping. Observe the inner signs.

Finally,

> Now the air energies are dissolving into the mind energies. Your breath is ceasing. Observe the inner signs.

In this way the ritualist observes the outer signs and prompts the dying person to remain aware of the inner ones, giving the admonition, 'O one of noble character, do not let your mind wander.' If the dying person is a lama, address him with a term of respect. If he is an ordinary person, use his ordinary Buddhist name. Then with a gentle and clear tone speak these words,

> Pay heed, one of noble character. The time of your death has come. Keep your mind clear and alert. Pay heed. As you enter the death state, meditate on love, compassion and the enlightenment aspiration. Generate the thought, 'For the benefit of all living beings I will achieve peerless enlightenment.'
>
> In particular, generate the strong resolve that for the benefit of all beings you will recognize the clear light of death as the

> *dharmakaya,* and will accomplish the siddhi of *mahamudra* enlightenment in order to be of benefit to all living beings.
>
> Moreover, resolve that if buddhahood is not gained when the clear light arises and you must enter the bardo, then you will recognize the bardo as the bardo (and not be drawn into the illusory experiences and appearances). Resolve to transform that bardo body into a buddha form with realization of *mahamudra* integration, and then manifest countless forms to help those to be trained, bringing benefit to living beings as vast in number as the measure of space.
>
> In this way resolve never to become separated from the bodhisattva resolve of universal goodness in accordance with the instructions received during life.

These words should be read clearly and gently, with your lips close to the ear of the dying person.

If the dying person is a high lama or advanced practitioner, then when the breath ceases you should pronounce the following,

> Now death is upon you, and the clear light of death about to arise. Remember the appropriate meditation practice and apply it now.

For all others read as follows,

> Pay heed, O child of noble character who is called Such-and-Such. Listen well. The pure clear light of the *dharmata* is now arising. Please recognize it. O child of noble character, this pristine state of consciousness that you now experience has no limiting factors such as parts, isolates, or colour. It is in nature the pure void itself. It is the *dharmata* in the nature of the All Good Female Buddha Samantabhadri, the emptiness nature of your own mind. But it is not an emptiness that is a mere nothingness; rather, it is the unobstructed radiance of your own mind, in the nature of the

All Good Male Buddha Samantabhadra. It is the void that is the non-inherent nature of your own mind, inseparable from and non-dual with the primordial radiance of that same mind. Thus is a Buddha's indivisible *dharmakaya*.

Rest within this great sphere of light that is the non-duality of the radiance and void nature of your own spirit, and become a radiant Amitabha Buddha beyond birth and death.

Merely recognizing where you are at this time is sufficient. This aspect of your mind is utter purity itself. Know it as the Buddha. Beholding this aspect of your own mind is sufficient to induce buddhahood.

These words should be recited clearly three or seven times. The first recitation will remind the dying person of the instructions that were received from the guru during his lifetime. The second recitation will point out the nature of his own mind and the clear light consciousness. The third will cause this awareness to transform into the *dharmakaya* and achieve liberation.

This is the first pointing-out of the clear light of death. If the radiance is not recognized, then after some time, maybe a bit more than the time it takes to eat an evening meal, a second radiance will occur. The energies leave (the central channel) and diffuse to either the right or left, and consciousness becomes very clear. How long this takes depends on how much positive or negative karma the person accumulated, and whether he had developed a strong meditation practice or not.

At that moment the consciousness leaves the body, but the person is not really aware if he is dead or not. He is outside the body, but can see it clearly, and can hear the cries of loved ones.

Facing page: *Menri Trizin Senge Tenzing, abbot of the Bon Monastery, Tashi Menri Ling in Dolanji, India, instructing disciples in the practice of* powa.

Following pages: *Statues of the Buddha sit with left hand in the meditation posture and the right in the earth-touching gesture, calling the universe as witness to enlightenment. Swayambhunath, Nepal, 1989.*

Pointing Out the Bardo of Truth

The forceful karmic projections have not yet begun to occur, and the terrifying appearances of the Lord of Death have not yet arrived. This is another excellent time to apply the instructions. Here practitioners will be of two basic levels: accomplished in the generation stage yogas (i.e. mandala meditation, mantra recitation, visualization, etc.); and accomplished in the completion stage yogas (i.e. the higher yogas that bring control of the chakras, pranas, and so forth). If the latter is the case, then his name should be called three times, and the reminder to immediately apply the yogas and recognize the radiance should be made.

If, on the other hand, the deceased had only been proficient in the generation stage of tantric training, then he should be instructed to visualize himself as his mandala deity and meditate on his tantric mandala.

The ritualist states as follows,

Tangka painting of the forty-two peaceful buddha forms that appear during the first seven days of the bardo experience. Nepal, 1997.

> O child of noble character, please meditate now on yourself as being in the form of your mandala deity. Allow no mental wandering. Offer fervent prayers to your mandala deity. Meditate on this form as being insubstantial, as though it were pure light, like a moon reflected in a pool of water.

Thus those who only developed proficiency in the generation or first stage of tantric practice should be directed to meditate on their personal mandala deity.

If they have not developed stability in this first level of tantric practice (but had received some tantric initiations during their lifetime), then it is best simply to advise them to meditate on Avalokiteshvara, the great Buddha of Compassion.

In this way those unable to recognize that they are in the bardo will be made to understand their situation. Those who had received instruction during their lifetime but were weak in practice will be helped. Also, those who were strong in both learning and practice but died of a sickness that impaired their ability to meditate will also be benefited. This pointing-out will be very useful for them.

It will also be useful for those who had good training and practice but who broke their spiritual vows or weakened their tantric precepts.

It is best if they succeed in the yogic application during the first bardo (i.e. during the experience of the clear light of death), but if this does not happen they can also make a second attempt during the second bardo experience, which is known as 'the impure illusory body'.

At that time the method of blending mother and son clear lights should be applied. Then all darkness of past negative karma is dispelled, just like the rising sun dispels the darkness of the night.

During the so-called second bardo the deceased develops the sense of having a body. This might cause some confusion, and again an instruction should be read. However, the strong bardo visions and appearances have not yet begun to occur. Although the clear light that is the basis of all experience was not previously recognized, there is a possibility that it could be recognized here and liberation achieved.

If liberation is not achieved even in this second bardo stage, then the third bardo will arise, the so-called 'bardo of truth', and the bardo visions and appearances will begin to manifest.

It is most important that (the section of the *Bardo Todol* known as) *Liberation Through Hearing in the Bardo of Truth* be read at that time. It has great strength and will produce great benefits.[1]

The deceased is now separated from his body, but can behold the crying and lamenting of loved ones, the distribution of his possessions and so forth. He can see and hear everyone, but they seem unaware of his presence, and this disturbs his mind.

At this time he experiences sounds and light rays, and fearful images begin to appear. This is the time for reading the section known as *Liberation Through Hearing in the Bardo of Truth*. Call his name out, and then read with clear enunciation,

> Pay heed. O child of noble character, do not mentally wander. Make a strong effort to listen well. There are six bardo states: the bardo of natural birth and life; the dream bardo; the bardo of samadhi/dhyana; the bardo of the clear light of death; the bardo of truth; and the bardo of becoming.
>
> O child of noble character, you are now in the middle of experiencing three of these: the bardo of the clear light of death; the bardo of truth; and the bardo of becoming.
>
> The bardo of the clear light of death has come and gone, and you failed to retain it, and thus now wander here. Soon the bardo of truth and the bardo of becoming will arise. I will read the instructions to you. Please do not mentally wander, but listen well and recognize the situation.
>
> O child of noble character, the state known as 'death' has arrived, and you must leave this world. But you are not alone in this, for it happens to all. Stay free of attachment to what is being left behind. You cannot stay, nor can you take anything from this life with you. Whatever objects appear to your mind, have no attachments or aversions for them. Meditate on Buddha, dharma and *sangha*, and use them as your guides.

O child of noble character, no matter what appears in your mind, no matter how alluring or terrifying these images might be, simply remember these words and hold to their essential meaning as you travel in the bardo. This is a key to recognition and success.

Repeat the words, 'With all that appears during the bardo of truth, no matter how alluring or terrifying, I will recognize it all as mere emanations of my own mind. I will know that they are

only bardo visions and projections, and are mere appearances. Whatever gentle or violent appearances arise during this time of great significance, I will have no fear or apprehension.'

Recite these words in your mind and remain mindful of their meaning as you enter into the bardo of truth. This is very helpful in maintaining the ability to recognize the bardo visions that arise as being mere projections of one's own mind. Therefore do not forget them.

Lobsang Lama raises prayer flag above the clouds, Senchi Langma. Humla, Nepal, 1986.

The First of the Seven Phases of Unfoldment in the Bardo of Truth

'O child of noble character, your body and mind have now gone their separate ways. The bardo of truth will now appear, pure, radiant, and bright, like a shimmering mirage seen in a desert. Do not be afraid or intimidated. Recognize that it is a phenomenon arising in your own mind. Perhaps a great sound of truth will seem to come from within the light, like a thousand dragons roaring at once. Know that it is just the bardo of truth arising in your own mind, and have no fear or apprehension.

'Now you have a mental bardo body formed from your karmic tendencies, and not a body of flesh and blood. Therefore no matter what sounds, lights or forms appear, no harm will come to you. You cannot die from them. Simply know that they are expressions of your own mind, and are mere bardo appearances.

'O child of noble character, if you do not correctly recognize these appearances at this time and do not rely now upon this instruction, then

Buddha Vairochana and consort, who appear on the first day of the bardo experience, and inspire liberation from grasping at duality and separateness. Detail from tangka on page 169.

no matter how much you studied and practised during your lifetime as a human being, the lights will frighten you, the sounds will fill you with fear, and the forms will cause you to tremble. If you do not understand this instruction, then the sounds, lights and forms will cause you to run, and to wander into samsara.

'Pay heed, O child of noble character. After resting semi-consciously in this radiance for four-and-a-half days you will awaken and ask, 'What is happening to me?' Recognize that you are in the bardo. The norms of life as you knew them in the world no longer apply. Lights and forms manifest as visions.

'Everything seems to have a bluish hue, like the colour of the sky, and from the centre of this vast expanse of the pure realm of the sublime the Buddha Vairochana manifests. He is on a lion throne, his body is white in colour, and he holds an eight-spoked wheel in his hands. He is seated in sexual embrace with his consort Queen of Space, her body radiantly blue, and their lips tenderly touching.

'They symbolize the pure nature of your own *skandha* of consciousness, and they emanate a sky-blue radiance into all directions, representing the wisdom of the sphere of infinity.

'A blue radiance emanates from their hearts and comes to you, so bright that your eyes can hardly bear to look at it, shimmering with droplets and orbs of light. At the same time an alluring white light comes from the realm of the gods.

'Perhaps because of your previous negative karma you will feel discomfort and fear for the brilliant blue light and the wisdom of infinity that it expresses, and instead will feel an affinity toward the pleasant light from the god realms.

'Do not fear the brilliant blue light. It is the radiance of the wisdom of infinity of all the buddhas. Instead of apprehension, have veneration and respect for it. Think, "It is the light of the compassion of Buddha Vairochana, and I turn to it for inspiration."

'It is the radiance of Buddha Vairochana come to guide you through the path of the bardo. Do not be attracted to the dull white light of the god realms. Do not be allured by its pleasurable quality. Any attraction to it is just a reflex of your karmic instincts generated by mental fixation and ego-grasping. If you follow it, you will take rebirth in the realm of the gods. It is a doorway to samsara and an obstruction to liberation. Do not even look at it, but instead look to the brilliant blue radiance and offer this prayer to Vairochana:

> Kyema! Out of ignorance I wander in samsara.
> May the radiance of the wisdom of infinity be my guide.
> O Buddha Vairochana, lead the way.
> O supreme consort Queen of Space, hold me from behind.
> Show me how to cross the terrible path of the bardo.
> Point the way to the ground of perfect enlightenment.

'When this prayer has been offered with intense devotion, your bardo body will melt into rainbow light and you will transform instantly into a *sambhogakaya* buddha in the Vairochana pure realm of the sublime in the centre of the mandala.'

The Second of the Seven Phases of Unfoldment in the Bardo of Truth

Although this instruction is given, the forces of anger, negative karma and obscurations might cause him to fear the brilliant blue light. If this happens, then on the second day Vajrasattva Akshobya and his circle of buddha forms manifest, and negative karmic forces that can produce rebirth in the hells become active.

One pronounces the instruction, calling to the deceased by name.

'Pay heed, O child of noble character. Listen, and do not mentally wander. On this second day, the pure nature of the water element radiates forth as a white light. At this time from the pure realm of manifest joy in the east the Buddha Vajrasattva Akshobya manifests, his body blue in colour, a five-spoked *vajra* in his hand. He is seated on an elephant throne, and is in sexual union with his consort Buddha Vision, their lips tenderly touching. The bodhisattvas Kristigarbha and Maitreya are beside them, together with

Buddha Vajrasattva Akshobya, consort and entourage, who appear on the second day and bring liberation from anger. Detail from tangka on page 169.

the heroines Lasya and Pushpa, all in rainbow balls of light. These six buddha forms thus appear.

'They symbolize the pure nature of your own *skandha* of form, and they emanate a white radiance into all directions, representing the primordial mirror-like wisdom.

'From the heart of Vajrasattva Akshobya and consort comes a white radiance, brilliant and shimmering, so bright that your eyes can hardly bear to look at it, shimmering with droplets and orbs of light. At the same time a smoky light comes from the hell realms.

'Perhaps because of your previous anger and negative karma you will feel discomfort and fear for the brilliant white light and the mirror-like wisdom that it expresses, and instead will feel an affinity toward the smoky light of the hell realms.

'Do not fear the brilliant white light. It is the radiance of the mirror-like wisdom of all the buddhas. Instead of apprehension, have veneration and respect for it. Think, "It is the light of the compassion of Buddha Vajrasattva Akshobya, and I turn to it for inspiration."

'It is the radiance of Buddha Vajrasattva Akshobya and consort come to guide you through the path of the bardo. Do not be attracted to the dull smoky light of the hell realms. Any attraction to it is just a reflex of your karmic instincts of anger and aggression. If you follow it, you will fall to the hells and come to an unbearable suffering of heat, cold and weapons. It is a doorway to samsara and an obstruction to liberation. Do not even look at it, but instead look to the brilliant white radiance and offer this prayer to Vajrasattva Akshobya:

> Kyema! Out of anger I wander in samsara.
> May the radiance of the mirror-like wisdom be my guide.
> O Buddha Vajrasattva Akshobya, lead the way.
> O supreme consort Buddha Vision, hold me from behind.
> Show me how to cross the terrible path of the bardo.
> Point the way to the ground of perfect enlightenment.

'When this prayer has been offered with intense devotion, your bardo body will melt into rainbow light, and you will transform instantly into a *sambhogakaya* buddha in the Vajrasattva Akshobya pure realm of manifest joy in the east of the mandala.'

Gyandrak Gompa in the inner khorra, *Mt Kailash, Tibet. Gyandrak Monastery remains a destination for Bonpo and Buddhist pilgrims. It looms above the castle of the early Bonpo kings. The Buddhist Drigung Kargyu sect currently controls the monastery.*

The Third of the Seven Phases of Unfoldment in the Bardo of Truth

However, the forces of arrogance and greed are strong, and might cause negative karma and obscurations to dominate, in turn giving rise to fear of the brilliant wisdom lights and their hook-rays of compassion.

If this happens, then on the third day Buddha Ratnasambhava and entourage manifest. Simultaneously the light of arrogance and greed becomes active, as does the negative karmic force that can produce rebirth in the human realms. Again one pronounces the instruction.

'Pay heed, O child of noble character. Listen, and do not mentally wander. On this third day, the pure nature of the earth element radiates forth as a yellow light. At this time from the pure realm of great glory in the south the Buddha Ratnasambhava manifests, his body yellow in colour, holding a precious jewel in his hand. He is seated on a supreme horse throne, and

Buddha Ratnasambhava, consort and entourage, who appear on the third day of the bardo, and inspire liberation from arrogance. Detail from tangka on page 169.

is in sexual union with his consort Mamaki, their lips tenderly touching. The bodhisattvas Akashagarbha and Samantabhadra are beside them, together with the heroines Malaya and Dhupe, all in rainbow balls of light. These six buddha forms thus appear.

'They symbolize the pure nature of your own *skandha* of response/ feeling, and they emanate a yellow radiance into all directions, representing the primordial wisdom of equality.

'From the heart of Buddha Ratnasambhava and consort comes a yellow radiance, brilliant and shimmering, beautiful with droplets and orbs of light, so bright that your eyes can hardly bear to look at it. At the same time a pale blue light comes from the human realms.

'Perhaps because of your previous delusions of arrogance and greed, and your negative karma and obscurations, you will feel discomfort and fear for the brilliant yellow light and the primordial wisdom of equality that it expresses, and instead will feel an affinity toward the pale blue light from the human realms.

'Do not fear the brilliant yellow light. It is the radiance of the primordial wisdom of equality of all the buddhas. Instead of apprehension, have veneration and respect for it. Think, "It is the light of the compassion of Buddha Ratnasambhava, and I turn to it for inspiration."

'It is the radiance of Buddha Ratnasambhava and consort come to guide you through the path of the bardo. Do not be attracted to the pale blue light of the human realms. Any attraction to it is just a reflex of your karmic instincts of arrogance and greed. If you follow it, you will take rebirth in the human realms, and will experience the unbearable suffering of birth, sickness, old age and death once more. It is a doorway to samsara and an obstruction to liberation. Do not even look at it, but instead look to the brilliant yellow radiance and offer this prayer to Buddha Ratnasambhava:

Kyema! Out of arrogance and greed I wander in samsara.
May the radiance of the wisdom of equality be my guide.
O Buddha Ratnasambhava, lead the way.

O supreme consort Mamaki, hold me from behind.
Show me how to cross the terrible path of the bardo.
Point the way to the ground of perfect enlightenment.

'When this prayer has been offered with intense devotion, your bardo body will melt into rainbow light, and you will transform instantly into a *sambhogakaya* buddha in the Buddha Ratnasambhava pure realm of glory in the south of the mandala.'

The Fourth of the Seven Phases of Unfoldment in the Bardo of Truth

Some beings who have created much harm in their lifetime, have weakened their *samaya* precepts, and in general have cut themselves off from the root of good fortune, might be unable to achieve liberation, even though these words have been spoken. The forces of craving and attachment might arouse their negative karma and obscurations, and cause them to fear the brilliant wisdom lights and their hook-rays of compassion.

If this happens, on the fourth day Buddha Amitabha and entourage manifest. Simultaneously the negative radiance of craving and attachment become active, as do the karmic forces that can produce rebirth in the ghost realms. Again one pronounces the instruction.

'Pay heed, O child of noble character. Listen, and do not mentally wander. The fourth day is upon you. The pure nature of the fire element now

Buddha Amitabha, consort and entourage, who appear on the fourth day of the bardo, and inspire liberation from craving and attachment. Detail from tangka on page 169.

radiates forth as a red light. At this time from the pure realm of pure joy in the west the Buddha Amitabha manifests, his body red in colour, holding a lotus in his hand. He is seated on a peacock throne, and is in sexual union with his consort Pandaravasini, their lips tenderly touching. The bodhisattvas Avalokiteshvara and Manjushri are beside them, together with the heroines Ghirta and Aloke, all in rainbow balls of light. These six buddha forms thus appear.

'They symbolize the pure nature of your own *skandha* of distinguishing awareness, and they emanate a red radiance into all directions, representing the primordial all-distinguishing wisdom.

'From the heart of Buddha Amitabha and consort comes a red radiance, brilliant and shimmering, beautiful with disks of light, so bright that your eyes can hardly bear to look at it. At the same time a pale yellow light comes from the ghost realms.

'Perhaps because of your previous delusions of craving and attachment, and your negative karma and obscurations, you will feel discomfort and fear of the brilliant red light and the primordial all-distinguishing wisdom that it expresses, and instead will feel an affinity toward the pale yellow light from the ghost realms.

'Do not fear the brilliant red light. It is the radiance of the primordial all-distinguishing wisdom of the buddhas. Instead of apprehension, have veneration and respect for it. Think, "It is the light of the compassion of Buddha Amitabha, and I turn to it for inspiration."

'It is the radiance of Buddha Amitabha and consort come to guide you through the path of the bardo. Do not be attracted to the pale light of the ghost realms. Any attraction to it is just a reflex of your karmic instincts of craving and attachment. If you follow it, you will take rebirth in the ghost realms, and will experience unbearable suffering from deprivation, hunger and thirst. It is a doorway to samsara and an obstruction to liberation. Do not even look at it, but instead look to the brilliant red radiance and offer this prayer to Buddha Amitabha, holding him single-pointedly in your mind:

Kyema! Out of attachment and yearning I wander in samsara.
May the radiance of the all-distinguishing wisdom be my guide.
O Buddha Amitabha, lead the way.
O supreme consort Pandaravasini, hold me from behind.
Show me how to cross the terrible path of the bardo.
Point the way to the ground of perfect enlightenment.

'When this prayer has been offered with intense devotion, your bardo body will melt into rainbow light, and you will transform instantly into a *sambhogakaya* buddha in the Buddha Amitabha pure realm of pure joy in the west of the mandala.'

The Fifth of the Seven Phases of Unfoldment in the Bardo of Truth

It is almost impossible not to achieve liberation by this time. Nonetheless there are some beings that are unable to leave behind the instincts and mental associations with their attachments. The forces of their jealousy and envy, as well as their negative karma and obscurations, might cause them to fear the brilliant wisdom lights and their hook-rays of compassion.

If this happens, then on the fifth day Buddha Amoghasiddhi and entourage manifest. Simultaneously the negative radiance of jealousy and envy become active, as do the karmic forces that can produce rebirth in the titan realms. Again one pronounces the instruction.

'Pay heed, O child of noble character. Listen, and do not mentally wander. The fifth day is upon you. The pure nature of the air element now radiates forth as a green light. At this time from the pure realm of success in the

Buddha Amoghasiddhi, consort and entourage, who appear on the fifth day of the bardo, and inspire liberation from envy and jealousy. Detail from tangka on page 169.

north the Buddha Amoghasiddhi manifests, his body green in colour, holding a crossed *vajra* in his hand. He is seated on an eagle throne, and is in sexual union with his consort Samaya Tara, their lips tenderly touching. The bodhisattvas Vajrapani and Sarvanivaranaviskambhin are beside them, together with the heroines Gandha and Naivedya, all in rainbow balls of light. These six buddha forms thus appear.

'They symbolize the pure nature of your own *skandha* of karmic predispositions, and they emanate a green radiance into all directions, representing the primordial all-accomplishing wisdom.

'From the heart of Buddha Amoghasiddhi and consort comes a green radiance, brilliant and shimmering, beautiful with droplets and orbs of light, so bright that your eyes can hardly bear to look at it. At the same time a pale red light comes from the titan realms.

'Perhaps because of your previous delusions of jealousy and envy, and your negative karma and obscurations, you will feel discomfort and fear of the brilliant green light and the primordial all-accomplishing wisdom that it expresses, and instead will feel an affinity toward the pale red light from the titan realms.

'Do not fear the brilliant green light. It is the radiance of the primordial all-accomplishing wisdom of the buddhas. Rest within the sphere of equanimity, without attraction to some beings and hatred for others. Instead of apprehension, have veneration and respect for it. Think, "It is the light of the compassion of Buddha Amoghasiddhi, and I turn to it for inspiration."

'It is the radiance of Buddha Amoghasiddhi and consort come to guide you through the path of the bardo. Do not be attracted to the pale red light of the titan realms. Any attraction to it is just a reflex of your karmic instincts of jealousy and envy. If you follow it, you will take rebirth in the titan realms, and will experience unbearable suffering of conflict, war and defeat. It is a doorway to samsara and an obstruction to liberation. Do not even look at it, but instead look to the brilliant red radiance and offer this prayer to Buddha Amoghasiddhi, holding him single-pointedly in your mind:

Kyema! Out of jealousy and envy I wander in samsara.
May the radiance of the all-accomplishing wisdom be my guide.
O Buddha Amoghasiddhi, lead the way.
O supreme consort Samaya Tara, hold me from behind.
Show me how to cross the terrible path of the bardo.
Point the way to the ground of perfect enlightenment.

'When this prayer has been offered with intense devotion, your bardo body will melt into rainbow light, and you will transform instantly into a *sambhogakaya* buddha in the Buddha Amoghasiddhi pure realm of success in the north of the mandala.'

The Sixth of the Seven Phases of Unfoldment in the Bardo of Truth

When the five radiances have been pointed out in this way, it is almost certain that one will identify with and achieve liberation through at least one of them.

However, some beings fail to do so. Their lack of familiarity with recognizing the pure nature of the images that appear to the mind, their lack of wisdom, and their negative habits of mind will prevent them from holding on to the hooks of compassion of the radiances of the five buddhas. The brilliance and beauty intimidates them, and they wander away from it and fall downward.

Thus they fail to win liberation and enlightenment, and the bardo visions of the sixth day arise. On this day all five buddhas, together with consorts and entourages, will appear to them. Simultaneously the light rays of all six realms of the world shine forth.

One pronounces the instruction.

'Pay heed, O child of noble character. Listen, and do not mentally wander. Over the past five days the radiances of the five buddha families appeared to you, the pure natures of your own elements and *skandhas,* but because of the force of your karmic limitations you were unable to recognize them. If on any of these five occasions you had recognized the radiances as emanations of the pure nature of your own mind, and if you had allowed yourself to melt into rainbow light and dissolve into them, then you would have achieved full enlightenment as a *sambhogakaya* buddha in the according pure sphere.

'However, you were unable to recognize the radiances as emanations of your own pure nature, and were unable to dissolve into them, and thus you now wander here.

'Listen well and do not mentally wander. The radiances of the five buddha families, and also the radiances of what is known as the four unified wisdoms, have now come to your aid. Recognize them for what they are.

'O child of noble character, the pure aspects of the four physical elements appear as four radiances. At the same time, as before, in the centre of the vast sphere appears Buddha Vairochana with consort and retinue; Buddha Vajrasattva with consort and retinue appear in the eastern sphere; Buddha Ratnasambhava with consort and retinue appear in the southern sphere; Buddha Amitabha with consort and retinue appear in the western sphere; and Buddha Amoghasiddhi with consort and retinue appear in the northern sphere.

'O child of noble character, to the outside of these five buddha lords, consorts and retinues appear the four male and four female guardians of the doors, wrathful in appearance. Vijaya, Yamantaka, Hayagriva and Amritakundali are the males; Ahkusa, Pasa, Shrikhala and Ghanta are the females.

'There are also the six manifestations of the Buddha in the forms in which he emanated into the six realms in order to benefit the living beings dwelling therein: Buddha appearing as Indra to benefit the gods; Buddha appearing as Vemachitra to benefit the titans; Buddha appearing as the monk Shakyamuni to benefit human beings; Buddha appearing as Dhruvashinha to benefit animals; Buddha appearing as Jvalamukhato to benefit the hungry ghosts; and Buddha appearing as Dharmaraja to benefit hell beings.

'Buddha Samantabhadra appears, and his consort Samantabhadri, and then all forty-two deities of the *sambhogakaya* mandala.

'All of these buddha forms manifest from within your own heart and then appear to you as though outside. They are mere expressions of your own inner pure enlightenment nature.

'O child of noble character, these buddha forms and buddha-fields are not separate from you. The five buddhas and their retinues are the four directions of your heart, together with the centre of the four. They manifest from your heart, and are expressions of your own inner nature. Those forms are not external, but are the playful expressions of your own being, your own mind, spontaneously present from beginningless time. Know them as such.

'O child of noble family, words like big or small do not apply to the manner in which these buddha forms appear, for they are beyond such conventions. They manifest as a circle of five, each as a five-coloured mass of light, males as heroes and females as heroines, all appearing simultaneously as an integrated mandala. Know them as your tantric mandala deities, your objects of meditation, and as expressions of your own mind.

'O child of noble family, from the hearts of the buddhas of the five, male and female in sexual union, come forth lights of the four wisdoms in union, like a stream of sunbeams, and enter your heart. First from Vairochana and consort come the light-rays of the primordial wisdom of infinity; then from Vajrasattva Akshobya and consort come the light-rays of the primordial mirror-like wisdom; from Ratnasambhava and consort come the light-rays of the primordial wisdom of equality; and from Amitabha and consort come the light-rays of the primordial all-distinguishing wisdom. Each of the waves of light is immense, with droplets and orbs adorning it, filling all space, with no centre and no outer limit, as though one were inside an enormous glass bowl, of the colour associated with that particular buddha: Vairochana's clear like a mirror; Akshobya's like an upturned turquoise bowl; Ratnasambhava's pure gold; and Amitabha's ruby red. Each of the waves of light spins off countless orbs and droplets, those in turn emanating five radiances, filling the universe with brilliant wisdom.

'O child of noble family, these four buddhas (of the five) radiate in this manner. They are known as the four wisdoms combined. At this time

Amoghasiddhi's emerald green does not manifest, because the playful wisdom of your own enlightenment activity is not yet complete. Only when the other four have completed their transformations will the emerald light of fully enlightened playful activity manifest.

'The four are known as the four primordial wisdoms conjoined, and also as the path of the diamond hero. When these lights are blazing, remember the instructions received during your life from your gurus, and the glimpses of enlightenment achieved in practice. If you can do this, then seeing these radiances will be like seeing one's mother after a long parting, or seeing an old friend. Joy will arise, and this will encourage things to go in the right direction. This confidence will give birth to immutable enthusiasm for the path of the purity of *dharmata,* and will facilitate arousal of the powers of samadhi. This in turn will encourage absorption into the body of spontaneous awareness, and the attainment of the irreversible state of a *sambhogakaya* buddha.

'O child of noble character, together with the radiances of the wisdom radiances come light rays from the impure and illusory six realms: white for the god realms, red for the realm of titans, blue for the human realm, green for animals, yellow for hungry ghosts, and smoky for hell beings.

'These manifest at the same time as pure radiances of the primordial wisdoms. Do not be allured by them. Instead, place awareness in the depth of non-duality, without attraction or repulsion. Should you fear the wisdom radiances and be allured by the impure lights of the six realms, you will take rebirth as a being in one of the six realms, and again enter the terrible ocean of samsara with its hundreds of miseries, where there is no time for liberation.

'O son of noble character, if you have not received proper instructions from your gurus, fear of the brilliant wisdom lights could easily arise, and you could easily be allured by the impure lights of samsara. Proceed with care. Generate joy and enthusiasm for the brilliant wisdom radiances. Know that they are expressions of the five buddha families, come to guide you at this precarious time. Have no yearning for the six worldly lights, and keep the vision of the five buddhas and their consorts firmly in your mind. Offer the following prayer:

Kyema! Out of the five inner poisons I wander in samsara.
May the radiance of the four wisdoms conjoined illuminate my path.
May the five buddha lords lead the way.
May the five buddha consorts hold me from behind.
Show me how to cross the terrible path of the bardo.
Point the way to the ground of perfect enlightenment.'

Those of highest capacity who receive this pointing-out in the bardo directly recognize the nature of the wisdom radiances, merge with them, and achieve enlightenment on the spot. Middling practitioners rely upon faith and devotion, recognize the situation, and achieve liberation.

Lesser beings rely upon the power of heartfelt aspiration at this moment, and close the door to rebirth in a lowly and ordinary womb in any of the six realms. Thereafter they cultivate the four wisdoms conjoined, and gradually achieve enlightenment by means of the *vajra* path.

Buddhist chortens *dwarfed by snow-covered peaks. Zanskar, India.*

The Seventh of the Seven Phases of Unfoldment in the Bardo of Truth

In this way many beings will succeed by the pointing-out in the bardo when the peaceful visions arise.

However, there will be some who are heavily weighed down by their previous negative ways, or who have no training in or understanding of the ways of the spirit, or who have broken their tantric pledges. They will therefore remain very confused and will continue to wander downward on the spiritual ladder.

It is now the seventh day, and the Knowledge Holders (Vidyadhara) have come from the Dakini Pure Lands to rescue the wandering soul. At the same time lights emanate from the animal worlds produced by ignorance and instinctual behaviour. Therefore the ritualist calls the deceased by name and pronounces the instruction.

'O child of noble character, listen well and do not mentally wander. On this seventh day a pure and fierce five-coloured radiance shines within the sphere of the instinctual level of your mind. At this time the Knowledge Holders emanate from the Dakini Lands and come to rescue you.

'At the centre is a ball of rainbow light, and in it is the ripening Knowledge Holder known as the Peerless Lord of Dance, in sexual union with a red *dakini* holding a curved knife and a skull full of blood, her eyes gazing at the heavens.

'In the east of the mandala is the earth-dwelling Vidyadhara, white and smiling, in sexual union with a white *dakini*; in the south is the lord of longevity Vidyadhara, yellow and beautified with the marks and signs of excellence, in sexual union with a yellow *dakini*; in the west is the *mahamudra* Vidyadhara, red and smiling, in sexual union with a red *dakini*; and in the north is the naturally born Vidyadhara, green and with a menacing smile, in sexual union with a green *dakini*. All four *dakinis* hold a curved knife and a skull full of blood, and dance gazing at the heavens.

'Outside of these ten are an immeasurable number of *dakas* and *dakinis*. These include the *dakas* and *dakinis* of the eight charnel grounds, the four

Above: *The Knowledge Holders, consorts and entourage, who come from the Land of Dakinis on the seventh day of the bardo experience, to guide and liberate. Detail from tungka on page 169.*

families, the three worlds, the ten directions, and the twenty-four sacred power places.'

All the great male and female *dharmapalas* manifest in order to protect those who have kept their spiritual commitments and to punish those who have broken them. They wear the six kinds of ornaments made from human bone, and play tantric instruments such as hand-drums, thighbone trumpets, and drums made of skull cups. They wave flags and banners made from human skin, and burn incense made from human flesh. They are so vast in number that the whole universe seems to be filled, until the world itself seems to quiver and shake. Their musical instruments blast with sound and their dances fill all space.

At this time the instruction is pronounced.

'O son of noble character, you have entered the realm of unconscious instinct, where the pure innate wisdom shines with five radiances, like coloured threads braided together. Its intense radiance – luminous and clear – comes from the hearts of the five Knowledge Holders and enters your heart. It is so bright and dazzling that you can hardly bear to look at it. Simultaneously the dull green light of the animal world shines forth.

'The force of ignorance empowered by your karmic instincts might cause you to fear the brilliant wisdom light of five radiances, and cause you to be allured by the dull green light of the animal realms.

'Do not fear the five-coloured radiance. Recognize it as the primordial wisdom of the Knowledge Holders and their *dakinis* come to rescue you.

'Natural sounds of truth emanate from within the wisdom radiance, like the roar of a thousand dragons, resounding with the penetrating sound of wrathful mantras. Do not be intimidated, and do not flee. It is but playful theatre emanated by your own mind.

'Do not be allured by the dull green light of the animals. If you follow it, you will fall into the animal realms, where mental limitations and karmic instincts prevail, and will come to experience unbearable suffering. Do not be attracted to it. Look instead to the radiance of five colours.

'Meditate on Knowledge Holders and *dakinis*, and offer the prayer,

> O Knowledge Holders and *dakinis*, who have come to invite me to Dakini Pure Lands, look on me with compassion. My good karma is small, and I continue to plunge downward in the bardo. Although the five buddhas and their retinues had come to help, I failed to recognize them or to hold on to the hooks of their compassion. Show me the way now, before I fall further down. Inspire me to recognize the situation and to respond to your compassion.

'Thinking like this, hold the assembly in your vision single-pointedly and offer the following prayer,

> Kyema! Knowledge Holders and host of divine beings,
> gaze upon me.
> Out of great compassion please guide me on the path,
> For out of unconscious instinct I now wander in samsara.
> May the radiance of the primordial innate wisdom be my guide.
> O heroic Knowledge Holders, lead the way.
> O supreme consorts, you great *dakinis*, hold me from behind.
> Show me how to cross the terrible path of the bardo.
> Point the way to the Pure Land of the Dakinis.

'When these words are said, you will dissolve into a rainbow, merge into the hearts of the Knowledge Holders, and take instant rebirth in the Pure Land of the Dakinis. There is no doubt that this occurs. Advanced spiritual people easily recognize their situation at that time and succeed in the application. Even beings of strong negative karma can achieve liberation.'

This completes the first two sections of the *Bardo Todol*: recognizing the clear light of the moment of death; and recognizing the truth of the situation during the occurrence of the peaceful bardo visions.

Transition to the Second Week

In this way seven stages of unfoldment occur in the bardo of the path of truth. During these seven stages the various peaceful buddha forms manifest and attempt to lead one to liberation and enlightenment through the compassion of their wisdom radiances. Each phase provides opportunities for liberation, and most people will succeed in one of these seven days.

However, the forces of negative karma, delusions and obscurations are strong. Some will not recognize their situation or will fail to make the appropriate spiritual effort, even though the instruction is clearly read. Thus they will not gain liberation, and will continue to fall downward.

When this is the case, they will enter another cycle of seven days, which are days eight to fourteen in the unfolding bardo cycle. This time, however, the mind is more fearful than before, and also awareness is weaker. As a result the appearances take on a more sinister edge. Yet, there is one advantage.

From the sphere of pure luminosity, a dzogchen *lineage master embodies the natural perfection of being. Mustang, Nepal, 2005.*

They are so terrifying in appearance that the mind has no inclination to be distracted by anything else. The buddhas now emanate to guide one, but they appear in the form of the fifty-eight wrathful mandala deities.

If one does not apply the correct method for liberation at this time, no amount of ordinary spiritual learning will help. Peoples of oceanic Buddhist learning, famous monks, scholars holding the *khenpo* degree, great philosophers and debaters: all are equal to ordinary people at this time if they do not apply the method of liberation in the bardo. They are taken in by the appearances, sounds and terrors, are filled with fear, and then flee to their ruin.

Even a simple tantric yogi, however, may have an advantage. During his lifetime he will have cultivated meditation on the mandala deities, and developed a familiarity with the practices of visualization, mantra and the transformation of appearances. When he sees the buddhas appearing in wrathful forms he will recognize them as emanations of his own mind and see them as mandala meditation deities. Rather than fear he will experience joy, like meeting old friends, and will easily be able to apply the methods of transformation with confidence. At that time he will merge with them into the sphere of non-duality, and achieve buddhahood on the spot.

This is one of the many beneficial side-effects and blessings of tantric practice. Even if the yogi did not achieve maturity in actual practice, simply having received the initiation and having seen the mandala will generate a predisposition to respond positively in this way.

On the other hand, Buddhist scholars and teachers with no tantric experience will not have these blessings, no matter how learned they are or how well they can speak on dharma. Many auspicious signs manifest when even an ordinary tantrik passes away, such as rainbows in the sky, auspicious cloud formations and birds, and precious relic substances miraculously produced from his corpse or from the ashes of his funeral pyre. None of these signs appear for ordinary scholars and teachers. When they die they find themselves quickly out of their depths, and the wrathful appearances generate either fear or aggression within them. They then either flee or attack; but they are running from or attacking their own mental projections.

For those who have achieved high levels of meditation and realization during their lifetime on methods such as *mahamudra* and *maha ati,* it is perhaps not necessary to have the *Bardo Todol* read at the time of death. They will be able to respond appropriately to whatever arises without assistance. Their meditation experience will keep them appropriately centred and focused, and nothing extra will be required. For those on ordinary levels, however – even famous monks, scholars and teachers – a reading of the *Bardo Todol* is very useful indeed.

Those who recognize the clear light at the moment of death are able to achieve enlightenment directly and attain the *dharmakaya* aspect of enlightenment. Those who recognize the nature of truth itself during the appearance of the peaceful buddha forms achieve the *sambhogakaya* aspect of enlightenment.

Finally, those who recognize their situation during the appearance of the wrathful buddha forms and are able to merge with them will gain the blessings of the *nirmanakaya,* and as a result are able to take a positive rebirth where they can continue along the enlightenment path through tantric practice.

The Bardo of the Wrathful Manifestations

As for how the instruction is given in this phase of the bardo experience, the ritualist calls to the deceased by name three times, and then says,

'O child of noble character, pay heed and do not mentally wander. Previously you experienced the bardo of the peaceful appearances, but failed to perceive the situation and apply the methods for liberation at that time. Therefore you now wander here, and for the next seven days – the eighth to fourteenth phases of the bardo experience – the wrathful blood-drinking deities will appear to you.

'On the eighth day the lord of the buddha family manifests in the centre of your skull as Glorious Buddha Heruka and consort, his body deep red in colour. He has three heads, six arms and four legs, and stands in the centre of a blazing halo of light. Each face has three eyes, and his

Tangka painting of the fifty-eight wrathful buddha forms that appear during the second cycle of seven days of the bardo experience. Kham, Tibet, 1989.

eyebrows flash with lightning. His fangs are bared and he laughs thunderously, his yellow hair streaming upward . . .[1]

'O child of noble family, do not be intimidated or frightened, for he is an emanation of your own mind. See him as your own mandala deity, for in reality he is Buddha Vairochana and consort. Liberation is achieved the moment you understand this truth.'

When this has been said, the deceased recognizes the situation and merges inseparably with the appearance, instantly becoming a *sambhogakaya* buddha.

'On the ninth day the lord of the *vajra* family manifests in the eastern sphere as Power-Wave Vajra Heruka, his body dark blue in colour. He has three heads, six arms and four legs, and stands in the centre of a blazing halo of light. Each face has three eyes, and his eyebrows flash with lightning. His fangs are bared and he laughs thunderously, his yellow hair streaming upward as he embraces his consort . . .

'O child of noble family, do not be intimidated or frightened, for he is an emanation of your own mind. See him as your own mandala deity, for in reality he is Buddha Vajrasattva and consort. Liberation is achieved the moment you understand this truth.'

When this has been said, the deceased recognizes the situation and merges inseparably with the appearance, instantly becoming a *sambhogakaya* buddha.

'On the tenth day the lord of the *ratna* family manifests in the southern sphere as Power-Wave Ratna Heruka, his body dark yellow in colour. He has three heads, six arms and four legs, and stands in the centre of a blazing halo of light. Each face has three eyes, and his eyebrows flash with lightning. His fangs are bared and he laughs thunderously, his yellow hair streaming upward as he embraces his consort . . .

'O child of noble family, do not be intimidated or frightened, for he is an emanation of your own mind. See him as your own mandala deity, for in reality he is Buddha Ratnasambhava and consort. Liberation is achieved the moment you understand this truth.'

When this has been said, the deceased recognizes the situation and merges inseparably with the appearance, instantly becoming a *sambhogakaya* buddha.

'On the eleventh day the lord of the lotus family manifests in the western sphere as Power-Wave Padma Heruka, his body dark red in colour. He has three heads, six arms and four legs, and stands in the centre of a blazing halo of light. Each face has three eyes, and his eyebrows flash with lightning. His fangs are bared and he laughs thunderously, his yellow hair streaming upward as he embraces his consort . . .

'O child of noble family, do not be intimidated or frightened, for he is an emanation of your own mind. See him as your own mandala deity, for in reality he is Buddha Amitabha and consort. Liberation is achieved the moment you understand this truth.'

When this has been said, the deceased recognizes the situation and merges inseparably with the appearance, instantly becoming a *sambhogakaya* buddha.

'On the twelfth day the lord of the karma family manifests in the northern sphere as Power-Wave Karma Heruka, together with the colour goddesses, *dakinis,* and power goddesses. He stands in the centre of a blazing halo of light, and each face has three eyes. His eyebrows flashing with lightning and fangs bared, he laughs thunderously, his yellow hair streaming upward as he embraces his consort . . .

'O child of noble family, do not be intimidated or frightened, for he is an emanation of your own mind. See him as your own mandala deity, for in reality he is Buddha Amoghasiddhi and consort. Liberation is achieved the moment you understand this truth.'

When this has been said, the deceased recognizes the situation and merges inseparably with the appearance, instantly becoming a *sambhogakaya* buddha.

Most people will achieve liberation in one or another of these phases. The lessons learned during life, and the instruction read at the time of death, will enable them to recognize the situation and merge with the buddha mind.

Perhaps the fearsome visions will frighten them at first, but they will gradually recognize the situation and the fear will transform into wisdom – just as a fabricated lion might at first frighten a person, but once he sees the lion for what it is, the fear evaporates and turns into laughter. Here the fear turns into wisdom. The son-like clear light meditation that was cultivated during one's lifetime merges with the mother-like clear light that is the primordial nature of one's own mind. The self-liberating force of the flow of consciousness is naturally released, and one instantly becomes a buddha.

However, if he does not receive liberation, the following will occur:

'First the eight blood-drinking "white" goddesses will appear: four each in the cardinal and intermediate directions of your skull; white in the east, yellow in the south, red in the west, and so forth. Do not be afraid of them, but recognize them as appearances of your own mind.

'Then the eight multicoloured blood-drinking *dakinis* of the eight great charnel grounds will come, each with a different animal head: lion, tiger, fox, wolf, vulture, hawk, eagle and owl. Again, one manifests in each of the cardinal and intermediate directions, and each carries her particular symbolic hand implements. Do not be afraid of them, but recognize them as appearances of your own mind . . .

'The four blood-drinking goddesses of the gates will also manifest: white tiger-headed in the east; yellow pig-headed in the south; red lion-headed in the west, and green snake-headed in the north.

'O child of noble character, after these thirty wrathful blood-drinking buddha forms have manifested, and if you still have not achieved liberation, then the twenty-eight yoginis will manifest: six in the east, six in the south, six in the west, six in the north, and four guarding the four gates. These twenty-eight are but playful energies spinning off from the five buddha families manifest as the five *herukas*: buddha, *vajra*, *ratna*, *padma*, and karma.

'O child of noble character, the *dharmakaya* sends out countless emanations to benefit beings. Here it has manifested first as the forty-two peaceful buddha forms, and now as the fifty-eight wrathful buddha forms. If at any time you recognize that these manifestations and visions are but expressions of your own primordial luminosity, and are projections of your own mind, and if you merge with them into the sphere of non-duality, liberation will be instantly achieved.

'However, if you do not recognize them, then you will fear them because of their terrifying appearances and will flee. In this way you will continue to fall downward into realms of suffering . . .

'O child of noble character, no matter how much Buddhist learning or practice you have accumulated during your lifetime, if you have not developed the wisdom to see these manifest forms as your own projections, and as radiance from the five buddha families, you will not awaken from the sleep of the duality-grasping ignorance. But if you recognize this great secret of secrets for a single moment, you will instantly accomplish the liberation of buddhahood.

'If you fear the apparitions, they will become enormous and even more terrifying, filling all of space, and seeming to hold the history of karmic deeds in their hands, and terribly punishing those who have created great evils.

'Child of noble character, do not fear them, for your body now is but itself a mental projection and cannot be harmed. It is but a shimmering reflection of emptiness itself. Even these beings who manifest in the form of the Lord of Death are but emanations of your own mind.

'Similarly the assembly of peaceful and wrathful deities are but emanations of your own radiance. The moment you see this clearly, all fear evaporates and liberation arises naturally. Then merging into the sphere of non-duality with them, you instantly become a buddha.

'You should think that all the forms that appear are but emanations of the five families of buddhas come to assist you, and receive inspiration and guidance from them.

'Remember and meditate upon your own mandala deities, and request them for blessings and inspiration. Also remember and meditate upon your gurus, and call to them for their guidance.

'Call out with this prayer,

> Kyema! Out of unconscious karmic instinct I now wander in samsara.

May the radiance of the primordial innate free me from all fear.
O peaceful and wrathful deities, lead the way.
O supreme consorts and great *dakinis,* hold me from behind.
Show me how to cross the terrible path of the bardo.
Point the way to the state of buddhahood itself.

When countless empty images appear as peaceful and wrathful forms
May the buddhas hold me with the hooks of their compassion.
When the five great radiances arise,
May I recognize them as my own mental projections.
When the peaceful and wrathful deities appear,
May I remain strong and without fear.

When the force of my own negative karma brings pain,
May my mandala practice hold me free.
When great thunderous sounds arise in the bardo,
May I hear only *om mani padme hum,* the mantra of compassion.

May I rely upon Avalokiteshvara, Buddha of Compassion.
May I rely upon samadhi, the meditation on inseparable bliss and void.
May I see the five elements as friends, and not as enemies.
May I see right now the realms of the five buddhas.'

This passage should be repeated three or seven times by the ritualist. If the deceased hears them, he will certainly attain liberation.

People with no or little training during their lifetime in the methods for recognizing the innate nature of the mind will have a difficult time in the bardo. The better the training during life, the better will be the results that carry over into the bardo.

Those who had achieved deep meditation and gained basic experience of the clear light mind while alive, but who failed to achieve full enlightenment, will be able to rest within the clear light that arises at death and attain enlightenment then. Those on lesser levels, who developed maturity in mandala practice and visualization, can easily succeed when the peaceful and wrathful visions arise.

This teaching should be remembered and contemplated three times a day. It should be held so close to the heart that one would not lose thought of it even if a hundred assassins were suddenly to attack. It is so powerful that it has the strength to purify even the most negative of karmas, including the five inexpiable deeds. It should be learned when alive, and read beside one's bedside at the time of one's death.

What good fortune to meet with this greatest of doctrines, the very essence of the teachings of the Buddha.

Thus ends the instruction on the bardo of the path of truth.

Entering the Bardo of Becoming

Although the nature of reality was pointed out many times in this way during the bardo of *dharmata,* some people will nonetheless be overpowered by their own negative karma, will be obsessed with fear, and will fail to achieve liberation.

For this reason from the tenth day onward the following section of the *Bardo Todol* should be read to them,

'O child of noble character, pay heed. After death, people of very positive karma almost instantly find themselves in the god realms and those of very negative karma almost instantly find themselves in the hell realms.

'Those of intermediate karma find themselves in the bardo, where they wander until they find the appropriate place of rebirth. This has happened to you. You have experienced the visions of the peaceful and wrathful buddha forms in the bardo of *dharmata,* but failed to recognize the situation, and you fainted with fear. You awoke from the faint to find yourself wandering in a bardo body. It seemed to you much like your old body although it had some additional characteristics. As is said in a scripture, "The bardo body seems like a normal physical body of the past and future, with all senses intact, but

possessing miraculous powers and clairvoyance, such as the visionary perception of a god."

'The meaning here is that the bardo body at this point is a mental construct created by the memories of the body of the previous life, and resembles it. However, it has numerous exalted qualities, such as a sublime radiance. In addition it is free from any physical faults you might have had, such as blindness, deafness, scars and so forth.

'At this time you will be able to see your future rebirth, and will experience something of that realm. Those destined for rebirth as a particular god will perceive the heaven associated with that type of god.

Above: Dakas *and* dakinis, *manifestations of the wrathful buddha forms, utilize skilful dance movements to entice the deceased to turn towards liberation and enlightenment. Detail from tangka on page 209.*

The same is the case with those moving toward rebirth as a titan, ghost, hell being, animal or human.

'Another meaning of "past and future" in the above scriptural quote is that for some days you have a sense of inhabiting a physical body that resembles that of your previous life, while thereafter the sense of your body begins to resemble the body of your future life.

'It is most important at this time to relax the mind in the sphere of the void, without grasping or rejecting. Rest in the pure luminosity of your own awareness as taught by your gurus during your lifetime. Liberation will be gained and rebirth in a womb avoided.

'If you do not have this ability, then visualize your gurus in the form of your mandala deity and generate strong feelings of faith. This will help. Those who have not generated the wisdom of the void can simply rest in the sphere of devotion.

'As mentioned above, your bardo body is free of all ordinary physical faults. It also possesses miraculous powers. You can fly, walk through walls, levitate and so forth without any difficulty. These are signs that you are dead and are in the bardo.

'O child of noble family, you can see your home, family and friends. They seem remote and dream-like. You might speak to them, but they do not seem to hear and do not answer you. You see them crying over your passing, and you understand that you are dead. This causes intense pain, like a fish thrown on hot sand.

'Do not be attached to relatives, friends and loved ones at this time, for they can no longer help you. Instead, meditate on your gurus and mandala deities, and call to Avalokiteshvara, the Buddha of Compassion, and your pain and fear will evaporate.

'O child of noble family, the winds of your past karma are now blowing wildly, and your mind rides on them like a man on a horse. Your mind is like a feather in a windstorm, moving in whatever direction the karmic winds blow it. You look at the loved ones lamenting your death, and you know you are now dead, which causes you grief. But do not feel sad or disturbed, for death comes to all, and is but a state of transition from one reality to another.

'The world around you seems somewhat greyish, like the period between day and night in autumn. It is the bardo, and will last for two, three, four, five, six or even seven weeks. In total it can continue for forty-nine days. For most people it lasts about three weeks, but the exact length varies in all people because of individual karma.

'O child of noble family, the winds of karma will drive you from behind, and a thick darkness will seem to lurk in front of you. Terrible sounds and visions will emerge from the darkness. Do not fear any of this, for it is all your own mental projection. You will sense animals and harmful people chasing you. The four elements will also challenge you, with sounds of mountains crumbling around you, lakes and rivers flooding, fires engulfing you and windstorms attacking you.

'Terrible precipices will appear on all sides. Their colours are white, red and black, for they are projections of your own attachments, aggressions and mental darkness. Recognize them for what they are, and call to the gurus and the Buddha of Compassion for guidance and inspiration.

'At this time those of strong positive karma and meditation training will mostly experience pleasant visions, those of strong negative karma will mostly experience terrible and fearful visions, and those in between will experience apathy and darkness.

'O child of noble character, no matter what appears to you, do not be allured or fearful. Call to your gurus, the Three Jewels of Refuge, and the Buddha of Compassion. Rest the mind in the blissful *mahamudra* state with no pushing or pulling.

'O child of noble character, houses and temples might appear to you, and you will attempt to rest and find warmth in them. But they can offer no respite, for the karmic winds will continue to push you on. Do not seek a shelter, but instead rest the mind in its own primordial radiance.

'Food and companionship only sporadically appear, and pleasure and pain seem to arise randomly. These are signs that you are in the bardo of becoming.

'You will see your home and loved ones, and even your own corpse. This will cause you to realize that you are dead. You might even try to re-enter your old body. But it cannot be revived, and you cannot dwell in it for long.

It will now be frozen by the winter cold, made putrid by the summer heat, or perhaps even buried or cremated by your loved ones, or offered as a gift of food to the birds or wild animals, for many days have now passed since your death occurred. Mountains of despair will press on you from all sides.

'Drop all yearning and fear, and rest in the *mahamudra* state without distraction.'

Liberation should easily be achieved when the pointing-out is read in this way. However, if the deceased still fails to exhibit signs of release then the ritualist should call to him by name and speak as follows,

'O child of noble character, Such-and-Such by name, pay heed. Your difficulties are being created by your own karma, so do not point the blame elsewhere. Call to your gurus and the Three Jewels for guidance and inspiration. Meditate on your mandala deities, and rest in the primordial *mahamudra* awareness.

'Otherwise your own sense of good and bad will arise, and you will remember all the good and bad that you have done. The terrible Lord of Death will seem to appear, and as you recollect your life he will pile up white and black pebbles on a scale. You will be filled with fear, and will attempt to rationalize, but to no avail. He will hold up a mirror, and all will be reflected just as it occurred.

'When the scale is filled with black pebbles the Lord of Death will laugh, and will drag you away, where his minions will cut and rip you into pieces, eat your flesh, drink your blood and gnaw on your bones. You will feel terrible fear and pain, but will be unable to die, for it is only your own mental projection, a theatre of your own conscience. Again and again they will kill you in this way, but you will instantly revive and the terror will continue.

'O child of noble character, when the Lord of Death appears, you need have no fear of him. Your bardo body is a mental construct and cannot be harmed or killed. It is but a mental projection cast in the field of pure emptiness. The Lord of Death also is void of real being, and is a mere projection of your own mind. The void cannot destroy or harm the void. A non-existent thing cannot harm another non-existent thing.

'When you wander in the bardo, all the gods, ghosts and demons that appear to your mind are but your own mental projections. They have no existence whatsoever apart from their nature as fantasies. Recognize them as mere bardo appearances, and rest the mind in *mahamudra* awareness.

'If you lack the power of samadhi that serves as the support of *mahamudra* awareness, then look closely at the projections that appear and notice their void nature. This awareness of the void nature has the quality of *dharmakaya*. The reverse side of the awareness of voidness is the radiance of the blissful mind perceiving the void. This is the *sambhogakaya*.

'Voidness and radiance are not separate entities, but are two aspects of the same phenomenon. Similarly, *dharmakaya* and *sambhogakaya* are indivisible entities. Voidness by nature is radiance, and radiance is voidness.

'When mind dwells spontaneously in the inseparability of these two – the void and the radiant natures – and arises nakedly in the unborn state, this is the experience of the *svabhavakaya*.

'Conversely, the *nirmanakaya* is the inseparable void and radiant natures manifest universally, without any obstruction or lapse, as an expression of compassion.

'O child of noble character, if you can see the flow of these four enlightenment qualities within your own mind, the enlightenment of the four kayas will be instantly achieved.

'The difference between an enlightened and an unenlightened being comes down to this one simple dynamic: seeing and not seeing the four kayas within yourself. As a scripture puts it, "In an instant comes fragmentation. In an instant comes complete enlightenment."

'O child of noble character, until now the bardo visions have appeared, but you have not recognized them for what they are, and have responded with fear. Be careful. The rope of the compassion of the buddhas could be severed, and you could fall far from liberation.'

Most will be liberated when these words are spoken. However, if some have no training whatsoever, they might fail to grasp the moment. When this is the case, the following words should be spoken,

'O child of noble character, remember your gurus and the Three Jewels, and meditate on your mandala deities as being an embodiment of them. Recollect the Buddha of Compassion, and remember your initiation name received during your lifetime. Say it aloud to the Lord of Death. Remember that you cannot be harmed.

'Do not respond with fear or aggression to anything that you experience. It is easy to oscillate between joy and sadness, but these emotions will only distract you.

'Have no attachments to the people or possessions left behind. Feel no anger for those who inherit and now relish your property. This will only cause rebirth in the hells or as a ghost. You can no longer benefit from those things, so renounce them in your mind. No matter who is enjoying them now, meditate that you offer them to the Three Jewels of Refuge. Rest the mind in non-attachment.

'Rituals might be offered for your benefit, and you might feel agitation over any errors made in their performance, or anger because some of the ritualists seem lazy or sloppy. These thoughts cannot help. Instead think that the minds of the ritualists are Buddha-mind, their chanting is Buddha-speech, and their bodies are Buddha-body. Maintain pure thinking in this way. If you can do so, then even if negative karma is pushing you down to the lower realms you will immediately feel happiness, and the wave of joy will cause the course of your evolution to be reversed, so that you will instantly move toward a higher rebirth. Therefore make every attempt to avoid negative thoughts at this time.

'O child of noble character, your mind has no physical support at this time, so the nature of your thoughts is very important. Do not entertain negative thoughts or dwell upon memories of negative deeds, but instead remember the positive things of your life, the sources of good karma. Generate faith and devotion for your gurus and the Three Jewels of Refuge, and offer prayers to your mandala deities and the Buddha of Compassion. Make the following aspiration,

Now I am parted from my loved ones,
And alone I wander in the bardo.
My own projections appear to my mind.
O compassionate buddhas, send hooks of compassion
And free me from the terrors of the bardo.
O mandala deities, eliminate my anxiety.

When the sounds of truth in the bardo
Resound like the bark of a thousand dragons,
May I hear these as *om mani padme hum,*
The six-syllable mantra of compassion.
May the Buddha of Compassion inspire me
And the samadhi of bliss and light be my support.'

The Lights of the Six Realms of Rebirth in the Bardo of Becoming

Many will attain liberation when this has been said. For some, however, the forces of negative karma will be too strong and they will not succeed. When this is the case the ritualist should continue. Calling the deceased by name he says,

'Pay heed, O child of noble character. You have not yet recognized the situation and gained liberation. As a result your sense of your body will begin to transform. Up to now it had resembled your body of your past life, but now this sense begins to fade, and it begins to become more like the body you are moving toward in your future life. You will feel a deep melancholy, and will begin to yearn for a new body. Driven by this force, you will wander to and fro.

'At this time you will become aware of six radiances. These are the lights of the six realms of worldly existence. The light from the realm toward which you are unwinding seems most strong.

'What are the six lights? There is the white light of the god realms, the red light of the realms of the titans, the blue light of the human realms, the green light of the animal worlds, the yellow light of the ghost realms, and the smoky light of the hells.

'You become more aware of the light of the realm toward which you are evolving, and your body takes on the hue of the light of that realm. You are at a crucial crossroads, so remember the instruction clearly.

'When one of the six lights begins to predominate, meditate that it is radiance from Avalokiteshvara, the Buddha of Compassion. This will change the direction you are taking, and will close the door to rebirth in that worldly realm.

'Now generate an image of yourself as assuming the form of your mandala deity, which is a similitude of the impure illusory body. Hold this for a while, and then dissolve this image of yourself into clear light, from the outside into the heart, and rest in this inconceivable sphere of the radiant void. Repeat the process many times: first arising as your mandala deity, retaining the image for a time, and then dissolving the self-as-mandala-deity image into radiant voidness.

'Even the sense of mind is dissolved into radiant voidness. Remember that mind pervades all of space, and has the nature of *dharmakaya*. Rest in this uncontrived state of *dharmakaya*, which is uncluttered by the duality syndrome that divides experience into self and other.'

Applying this meditation correctly at this point in the bardo will certainly prevent an undesirable rebirth and arouse the experience of liberation and buddhahood.

Avoiding an Inappropriate Rebirth by Preventing the Person from Moving in the Wrong Direction

Those who had but a weak practice of meditation in their lifetime might not succeed in the above application. They will remain in confusion and continue to wander in search of a womb. The ritualist should call to the deceased by name, saying,

'Pay heed, O Such-and-Such. Again you have failed to recognize the situation and failed to achieve liberation. Now the forces of karma are pressing heavily upon you. They are tossing you up, down and around in every direction. Remember Avalokiteshvara, the Buddha of Compassion, and recite his mantra.

'As before you will experience the terrors of the four elements in action: earthquakes, rushing waters, great fires and mighty windstorms. Snow and hail will whirl around you, darkness will close in upon you, and you will have the sense of being chased by humans, demons and animals.

Buddha manifests the fires of wisdom to close the door to the lower realms. Detail from tangka in Shechen Monastery. Nepal, 2006.

Those of weak karma will feel that they being forced to run to a place of misery, whereas those of positive karma will feel they are running to a happy place. Many signs of the place of the oncoming rebirth arise.'

Here there are two main methods to apply for preventing rebirth in an inappropriate womb: the method for stopping the person from moving in the wrong direction, and the method for closing the door of the womb. The ritualist reads,

'O child of noble character, whose name is Such-and-Such, visualize yourself as your mandala deity, radiant and insubstantial, free from the duality of separateness. If you have no tantric initiation into a mandala, then visualize that Avalokiteshvara, the Buddha of Compassion, appears before you. Then dissolve the entire visualized field into the radiant void from the outside melting in, and rest in the sphere free from conceptuality.'

This is the profound tantric method for preventing rebirth in an inappropriate womb by stopping the deceased person from moving in the wrong direction.

It can be supplemented with a more conventional method. Here the ritualist recites a verse of instruction:

> The bardo of becoming has dawned upon you.
> Keep your mind in single-pointed concentration
> Arouse your instincts of positive karma.
> Arouse the thought to persevere with a pure mind.
> Stay clear of distorted emotions, and
> Recollect the guru and his consort.

These words should be spoken clearly, so that the deceased can hear and be inspired by them.

'The line that says, "The bardo of becoming has dawned ..." refers to you being in the bardo. Observe the signs indicating that this is in fact the case. No reflection appears when you look in water, and your body casts no shadow. This is because your body lacks all substantiality, and is a mere mental projection, like a dream body.

'"Single-pointed concentration" means that you should be like a man on a horse who holds the reins firmly. Just as the horse will go wherever the rider indicates by a movement of the reins, in the same way your bardo experience will unfold in whichever way the mind moves. By controlling your mind you will control the experience. Hold the mind from moving in the wrong direction, and you will prevent the bardo experience from unfolding in the wrong direction.

'It is most important at this crucial time to focus the mind firmly without allowing any mental wandering. Arouse and hold firm your memories of the teachings, transmissions and initiations that you received while alive. This will activate the instincts of the positive karma you generated at that time.

'You can easily go up or go down on the ladder of rebirth at this moment, so hold the mind steady. A momentary lapse into negative thoughts or emotions could have catastrophic results. Concentrate single-pointedly.'

Five Methods for Closing the Doors to an Inappropriate Womb

The scriptures state, 'Close the doorways to rebirth in an inappropriate womb by means of joyous effort and pure thought.'

There are five methods for closing the doors to an inappropriate womb. In the first the ritualist calls out,

> O child of noble character, at this point in the bardo you will begin to experience scenes of men and women having sex together. You will want to join in with them, but restrain yourself. Instead, think that they are your guru and consort. Offer homage and make offerings in your mind, and request dharma teachings from them. Meditate intensely like this, and the door to the womb will be closed.

If this does not work and it seems you will soon enter an inappropriate womb, then apply another method. Here you should visualize the copulating couple as being your guru and his consort in the form of your

mandala deity and consort. Request them for blessings and *siddhis*. This too can close the door to the womb.

The third method is to be applied when strong thoughts of desire or anger arise. In general the scriptures speak of four kinds of birth: from a womb, from eggs, from heat, and miraculously. The first two are similar in terms of how they unfold in the bardo experience.

It is said that when the copulating couples appear to the person in the bardo, the bardo being generates sexual lust for one and anger toward the other. Anger and jealousy toward the male coupled with sexual desire and yearning for the female will produce rebirth as a male. Conversely, anger and jealousy toward the female coupled with sexual desire and yearning for the male will produce rebirth as a female. At that time you generate a sense of yourself as being the gender of your oncoming rebirth. Your sexual desire will cause you to identify with the copulating couple, and when the

Above: *Avalokiteshvara, the Buddha of Compassion, in sexual union with the goddess of song. Detail from a painting of the 100 peaceful and wrathful bardo deities. Shechen Monastery, Nepal, 2006.*

male experiences orgasm you will ride the energies of the blissful release. The intense bliss will cause you to swoon and lose self-awareness altogether, and you will eventually bond with the fertilized egg of the female.

If you enter a womb from the force of negative passions in this way, you will be reborn as a human or animal under inauspicious conditions. The fertilized egg will settle and grow in the womb, with your mindstream attached to it. You will then grow in the womb or egg, until you come out. Then you will open your eyes and see your new body. Perhaps it will be as a dog in a kennel, a pig in a pigpen, a cow or goat in a herd, or an ant or worm in the ground. It will then be difficult to climb back up the evolutionary ladder on the wheel of rebirth, and many lifetimes of suffering will follow. You will long wander through the six realms of rebirth, sometimes in the hell or ghost realms, sometimes in the various animal realms as an insect, fish, bird, reptile, mammal and so forth. Suffering and misery will follow life after life.

Therefore it is very important at this time in the bardo to avoid and reverse the forces of desire and anger. You should think to yourself, 'I have wandered in samsara for many lifetimes because of the forces of desire and anger. This will continue without end until I reverse these two negative forces. They are inner enemies causing me to drown in an ocean of misery. I will never again respond to these two negative emotions.'

Meditate single-pointedly in this way without any mental wandering. The door to rebirth in an inappropriate womb will automatically be closed.

However, if the doorway is still not closed one should engage the fourth method. Generate the thought that the various images and scenes that have appeared to you are illusory and insubstantial: the copulating couples, the earthquakes, floods, fires and windstorms, the terrible sounds and ferocious beings. All of these seem very real, but in reality are illusory bardo projections. They are like mirages; hallucinations and objects seen in a dream. Why have desire or anger for any of them? Why fear any of the images that arise in the mind? They only have the reality and power that you give to them, for they are your own mental constructs. The mind itself has no self-nature, so how can its projections?

Think to yourself, 'Until now I have believed the unreal to be real, the insubstantial to have substance, and have responded accordingly. Not seeing them as illusory, I ran from or followed them, and wandered in samsara. And I will continue to wander until I reverse this syndrome. Therefore I now acknowledge that they are mere illusions, like objects seen in a dream; like an echo of my own voice heard in a cave and believed to be the sound made by another; like hallucinations and mirages seen and believed to be real; and like the moon reflected in water that is mistaken for the actual moon. I will no longer accept these appearing phenomena at face value, but will meditate on their illusory nature.'

When the illusory nature is contemplated in this way, belief in the reality of appearances is undermined, and grasping at a solid self in one's own continuum as well as in seemingly external phenomena is relaxed. The resultant wisdom that arises automatically closes the door to the womb.

However, if even this does not close the door to inauspicious rebirth then one should rely upon the fifth method, which is the contemplation of the profound nature of the non-duality of the perceiving subject and the perceived object. The ritualist calls out,

> O child of noble character. Pay heed, and listen without mentally wandering. All things are of one nature with your own mind. That mind itself is void of self-nature, unborn and undying. The perceiving subject of mind and the objects that are perceived are of one nature, like water poured into water.
>
> Observe this aspect of your mind, and rest without any sense of duality in the primordial sphere. The doors to all four kinds of rebirth will certainly be closed.

Seeking an Appropriate Place of Rebirth

A variety of methods of gaining liberation in the bardo have now been read, and people of all levels of spiritual evolution will be able to succeed with one or another of them.

There are five good reasons why they will succeed. First, a bardo being has extrasensory perception, and thus will be able to clearly hear the *Bardo Todol* being read. Second, even a person who was deaf and dumb when alive will have all senses intact in the bardo, so will clearly hear and understand the reading. Third, the reading will be more pleasant and friendly to the bardo being than are the bardo visions, so he or she will certainly pay attention to the beautiful sounds and words. Fourth, the mind of a person in the bardo has no fixed abode or support, in the way an ordinary person is anchored by his or her physical body and possessions; for this reason the mind moves wherever the thoughts and mental focus guide it, and as a consequence can easily experience great transformations at the time. Fifth,

Lhamo Karmo, or Sitadevi, a female buddha who assists beings in finding an ideal place of rebirth. Mongolia, 2008.

it is said that the mind of a person in the bardo becomes nine times as intelligent as in normal life, so even the dullest person will be able to understand and apply the instructions when they are read.

It is said that the reading of the *Bardo Todol* should be continued for nine days. If liberation is not achieved on one of these nine, it almost certainly will on another.

However, some beings will be so controlled by their negative karmic patterns and delusions that they will fail to heed the instructions and thus fail to gain liberation. It will not be possible for them to close the doors to a rebirth in samsara. Therefore the only recourse is to assist them in finding an auspicious rebirth.

The ritualist should recite the words of refuge in the Three Jewels, supplicate the buddhas and bodhisattvas for inspiration and assistance, and then call to the deceased by name three times. He should then read the instruction.

'O child of noble character, Such-and-Such who has passed away, pay heed and listen without mentally wandering.

'Although many levels of instruction have been read to you, you have failed to grasp their import and to apply them successfully. You have failed to achieve liberation, and failed to close the doors to the wombs of rebirth.

'Therefore the time has now come for you to look to the task of choosing an acceptable womb for rebirth. There are several different instructions, so listen well without mentally wandering.

'O child of noble character, numerous signs of the land of your potential rebirth will appear to you. Choose an appropriate one for your rebirth.

'Beautiful lakes with geese and ducks will appear to those evolving toward rebirth in the eastern continent. Turn away from the temptation to go there, for although it has great prosperity, it is weak in spirituality. A lake surrounded with horses will appear to those evolving toward rebirth in the western continent. Again you should turn away from it, for although it is a land of many pleasures, it too is weak in spirituality. A lake surrounded with cattle and trees will appear to those evolving toward rebirth in the northern continent. Turn away from it, for although it is a land of great health and long life, it too is weak in spirituality.

'Fourth, a land with beautiful homes and towns will appear to those evolving toward rebirth in the southern continent. It is the best of the four continents for spiritual learning and practice, and so you should take rebirth there if you can.

'Those with the propensity to be reborn in the god realms will see beautiful temples adorned with jewels. This is an auspicious place for rebirth. Those with the propensity to be reborn in the realm of the titans will see beautiful forests and orchards, and also fire circles. This is an inappropriate place for rebirth, so turn away from it.

'Those with the propensity to be reborn in the animal realms will see caves, tunnels, fields and the like. These will appear dimly, as though looking through fog. Turn away and do not approach these places, for you will then be reborn as an animal.

'Those with the propensity to be reborn in the ghost realms will see a land characterized by desolation, like burned-out trees, dark earth, shallow caves and the like. Turn away quickly, for rebirth as a ghost is very undesirable.

'Finally, those with the propensity to be reborn in the hell realms will see a dark land with ugly red or black houses made of metal, black pits in the ground and dirty roads. Turn away quickly, for once you enter it is difficult to extricate yourself. Then you will be reborn in one of the hells and will experience great misery.

'O child of noble character, you are pressed from behind by the vengeance of your own karma, and dragged from in front by the assassins that are your own delusions. Fierce storms and terrible sounds attack from all sides. You try to hide in houses or caves, and fear leaving; and, staying hidden like this, you develop attachment to that inauspicious place. You will look for a body to enter as a means of escaping the terrors of the bardo, and can easily choose an inappropriate one.

'Here is the method to escape the terror. Visualize yourself as a wrathful mandala deity, perhaps Heruka, Hayagriva or Vajrapani, or as

your own personal mandala deity. Imagine your body as being very large and very strong, and that you are standing in the posture of subduing all negative forces. This will cause the terrifying visions to subside, and bring great waves of transforming power that enable you to look clearly for an appropriate place of rebirth. This is the principle of this tantric application.

'O child of noble character, the best method is to rest the mind in the sphere of *mahamudra* meditation. However, if you do not have the power to do this, then engage the tantric yoga of divine theatre that transforms all appearances into a divine abode, with self transformed into the mandala deity and all beings seen as *dakas* and *dakinis*.

'If even this cannot be done effectively, then avoid attraction and repulsion for the images that appear, and call on your mandala deity or on Avalokiteshvara, the Buddha of Compassion. This could bestow on you the power to become a *sambhogakaya* buddha even at this late stage of the bardo experience.'

Samantabhadra, the Buddha of All Perfections, in sexual union with the goddess of light. Detail from a painting of the 100 peaceful and wrathful bardo deities. Shechen Monastery, Nepal, 2006.

Two Methods for Taking Rebirth

As for how to choose the place of rebirth, there are two methods. One is for taking rebirth in a pure buddha-field, the other for taking rebirth in the impure world in an ordinary womb in order to continue dharma study, practice and work in the human realm.

The first is effected by generating the thought, 'Alas, how unfortunate I am. While countless others have achieved full buddhahood, or at least become *aryas* or *arhats,* I continue to wander lifetime upon lifetime since beginningless time in the muddy swamps of samsara. I am exhausted with samsara, and want no more of it. No more will I be reborn in the ordinary world. Instead I will rely upon Buddha Amitabha, who vowed to bring all beings that call upon him to Sukhavati, the Pure Realm of Joy. No more wombs or eggs for me! Instead I will take rebirth right now inside a lotus in Sukhavati.'

Rahula, protector of the Bardo Todol. *He symbolizes the power that causes temporary eclipses of the sun and moon, just like the power of death temporarily eclipses the life of a living being. Detail of a tangka in Shechen Monastery, Nepal, 2006.*

ར་ཧུལ།

Fix this thought clearly in your mind and hold firmly to it. You will instantly take rebirth in Sukhavati, Amitabha's pure paradise in the west.

Alternatively, there are numerous other buddha-fields into which you can take rebirth. For example, if you wish to be reborn in Maitreya Buddha's pure land of Tushita, generate the thought, 'I wish to take rebirth in Tushita, the pure land of Maitreya Buddha, and to sit in the presence of this illustrious lord of dharma.' This aspiration will instantly produce rebirth in Tushita.

The second method is for those who wish or are forced to enter a womb in the ordinary world. As earlier, look for the signs of the desired land of rebirth and choose the southern continent where dharma flourishes.

Then generate the thought, 'I wish to take rebirth in the human realm in order to be of great benefit to others. For this reason I will choose a rebirth in a body endowed with great merit, such as that of a universal emperor, where I can bring great benefits to others. Or I will be born as the son of spiritual teachers, tantric adepts, lineage holders or at least peoples of great spiritual enthusiasm.'

Holding this thought firmly in mind, you will see an appropriate and auspicious womb. Request the buddhas and bodhisattvas to bless it, and especially request Avalokiteshvara, the Buddha of Compassion, to send his blessings into it and transform it into a divine abode. Then enter it and take rebirth.

It is hard to tell what is the perfect womb for rebirth. Sometimes the power of bad karma and delusion will predominate, and it is easy then to see an inappropriate womb as good and an appropriate one as bad.

The only remedy is to generate the above thought of determination very strongly, and thereafter to rest the mind in the sphere beyond thoughts of good and bad, beyond wanting and dreading, beyond accepting and rejecting.

Not everyone can do this by himself, so to assist the deceased in reading the signs correctly the ritualist reads as follows:

> O child of noble character, whose name is Such-and-Such, try to avoid attachments and aversions in your search for an appropriate place of rebirth. No matter what appears to your mind, take refuge in the Three Jewels and in Avalokiteshvara, the Buddha of Compassion, and supplicate them for guidance and inspiration. Abandon for a moment all thoughts of the friends, relatives, loved ones and possessions left behind, and instead look to the radiances that appear. Choose the blue light of the human realm, or the white light of the god realms, and then fix your concentration upon it. These will lead you to rebirth in those auspicious realms.

This instruction should be repeated seven times. Afterwards, the ritualist should read whatever other bardo liturgies he can, such as *The Aspiration That Grants Protection in the Bardo.*

When this is done well, even the lowliest person can be assisted in finding an appropriate rebirth.

Conclusion

In general the most accomplished yogis will not have a bardo experience. They will effect a yogic transference of consciousness at the moment of death and bypass the bardo altogether.

The next most accomplished will recognize the *dharmakaya* nature in the clear light experience that arises after the dissolution of the elemental energies during the process of dying. They too bypass the bardo and go straight to buddhahood.

Everyone else must enter the bardo, and the best will achieve liberation in it. They will do so at their own level of the bardo experience. The specific level at which this will occur varies in accordance with personal talents and readiness, and the varying powers of individual karmic propensities and the delusions of the mind. The more elevated will achieve enlightenment sooner and the less elevated later.

Those of heavy negative karma and strong delusions will have to wander deeply into the bardo. However, on each level they will meet with

Lamas perform a reading in Bodh Gaya, India.

opportunities for release and liberation. For this reason the *Bardo Todol* provides many levels of instruction.

Some will fall even deeper, and for this reason the instruction on closing the doors to the wombs of the six realms is given. Finally, some will be so obscured by karma and delusion that even this is not possible; therefore the instruction on looking for an auspicious rebirth is provided.

Those with no training but strong faith in dharma should rely upon the power of refuge in the Three Jewels. Even the most pathetic practitioners can achieve a precious human rebirth complete with the eight freedoms and ten endowments by means of relying upon refuge in the Three Jewels. In the next life they will again meet with spiritual teachers and have the opportunity to develop their dharma practice.

When the *Bardo Todol* is read to someone who has entered the bardo of becoming, his positive karma is preserved and streamlined to the desired effect, like fixing a broken irrigation ditch saves the water from loss and delivers it to the desired field.

Even very negative people can benefit from having the *Bardo Todol* read at the time of their death, because the mind is very malleable in the death state and easily transforms. Only mental bodies exist at that time, so transformation is relatively easy. The compassion of the buddhas and the terrors of the bardo combine to bring about an attentiveness that such people might otherwise lack, and instant change becomes very possible. A heavy tree or a wooden machine that can only be carried by a hundred men easily floats down a river; in the same way, the waters of the bardo take away much of the weight of karma and delusion, and when the *Bardo Todol* is read that person is easily transported to a better place.

For this reason it is beneficial to read the *Bardo Todol* at the bedside of all who have died, regardless of whether they are high or low, good or bad, kind or cruel. All can be benefited from it.

As for care of the corpse, it should not be disturbed until the drops of blood and yellow fluid have been released from the nostrils. Loved ones should be discouraged from wailing and lamenting in its presence, at least for as long as the fluids are not released. No living beings should be sacrificed for the benefit of the deceased, but instead acts of good karma should be performed on the deceased's behalf, and the merit from these acts dedicated to a successful passage. It is also beneficial to read other related Buddhist scriptures for the benefit of the deceased.

It is useful to study the *Bardo Todol* during one's lifetime and become familiar with its meanings. At least one should familiarize oneself with it when the time of death approaches. If one is suffering from a terminal illness and cannot read it oneself, then having a dharma friend read it aloud at one's bedside is equally beneficial.

This profound doctrine can even produce enlightenment without practice or meditation. Merely seeing, hearing or reading it can cause the state of liberation to arise.

Even though this is true, it is also equally true that the better one knows the words and meanings of the text, the better the odds of obtaining maximum benefit from it. In this context, it is said that someone who can recite it without lapse or mentally wandering even while being chased by seven wild dogs will definitely achieve liberation and enlightenment during the experience of the clear light of death.

Were all the buddhas and bodhisattvas of the three times to search throughout the ten directions of the world, they would not find a more profound or beneficial doctrine.

Thus ends the *Bardo Todol*, or *Book of Liberation Through Hearing in the Bardo*, a revelation of the tantric adept Karma Lingpa while he was dwelling on Gampo Mountain. May it enrich both the enlightenment tradition and sentient beings, and cause every auspiciousness to increase.

Endnotes

PREFACE

1 Glenn H. Mullin, *Death and Dying: The Tibetan Tradition* (London: Penguin Arkana, 1987).

DEATH AWARENESS FOR A HAPPY LIFE

1 Atisha came to Tibet in 1042 and remained there until his death a decade and a half later. His impact transformed the landscape of Tibetan Buddhism, and all schools gradually adopted his approach. The present Dalai Lama once commented that although Tibetans find the Western expression 'Lamaism' somewhat obnoxious and prefer 'Tibetan Buddhism', if anything could be called Lamaism it would be the form of Buddhism introduced by Atisha, because his teachings became a basic foundation in all schools and sects.

2 Tib. *Jam-dpal-zhal-lung*. This is the Great Fifth's classic treatise on the *Lam Rim*, or Sutrayana meditations.

3 The Second was the greatest poet of the early Dalai Lamas. In this regard, he and the Seventh loom high above the other incarnations in the lineage. This verse is from his *Nyam Gur* or *Collection of Mystical Songs*.

4 Although many of the Seventh Dalai Lama's works in verse are spontaneous creations, some are written at the request of particular disciples. When the latter is the case, the name of the disciple is mentioned in the colophon. This particular poem is a long piece written at the request of his chief disciple, the illustrious Mongolian Lama Changkya Rolpai Dorje. The poem is one of several dozen in a collection titled *Lam Rim dang Lojong Nyam Gur dang Tshigchey* or *Songs and Verse Works to Transform the Mind*.

REINCARNATION AND THE WHEEL OF BECOMING

1 *See* pages 224-225.

2 In other words, the secret meaning is that the practice of the yogas associated with the peaceful and wrathful mandala brings enlightenment within a lifetime. The inner meaning is that by good living and control of the mind, and of the subtle energies at the time of death, one can attain a higher rebirth. On the outer level, merely reading the text to a dying person can help that person find liberation or an auspicious rebirth. *See* 'Karma Lingpa's Preface' on pages 142-144.

3 This is from a poem by the Seventh that was written for his chief disciple and dharma heir, the Mongolian master Changkya Rolpai Dorje. It is from the anthology entitled *Lojong Nyam Gur* or *Songs to Transform the Mind.* This verse is from that collection (my translation).

4 *Ibid.*

5 This disciple in particular is mentioned in the colophon to the poem as the 'Queen of Kyisho'. Presumably she was the wife of the Pakmo Drukpa patriarch, who at the time was a major player in central Tibetan political life. His wife seems to have been a very devout Buddhist, and a strong patron of the Second Dalai Lama.

6 The Seventh Dalai Lama, *op. cit.*

7 The Tibetan genre of text known as *Lo-rig* or 'Science of Mind' lists fifty-one mental/emotional factors: six primary mental/emotional distortions; twenty secondary negative mental states; eleven positive mind states; four factors that are sometimes positive and sometimes negative; five constantly present factors; and five factors facilitating perception/experience.

8 Shantideva's dates are uncertain. However, his *Bodhisattva-charya-avatara* is a very popular teaching manual with Tibetan lamas of all schools, and more than a hundred Tibetan commentaries to it written over the centuries. Its popularity continues, and the Dalai Lama has given week-long public discourses about it on over a dozen occasions, sometimes to crowds numbering in the hundreds of thousands.

THE TIBETAN BOOK OF THE DEAD AND THE THREE WAYS TO ENLIGHTENMENT

1 The Black and White Deities in the Tibeto-Mongolian pantheon are not positive and negative in the sense of bad and good, harmful or helpful, etc., nor in the sense of black and white magic. Rather, the idea is of black to remove obstacles and white to bring about desirable conditions. Both are under the Eternal Blue Sky, which in Buddhism became Samantabhadra, the primordial buddha who is the source or lord of the Mandala of 100 Peaceful and Wrathful Deities.

INDIAN MAHASIDDHAS AND THE CHARNEL GROUNDS CULTURE

1 Although India's population explosion in recent centuries has made the existence of charnel grounds impractical, the tradition nonetheless continues on a small scale in some communities, such as the Parsis of Maharashtra.

2 Karma Lingpa, the author or 'Treasure Revealer' of *The Tibetan Book of the Dead,* belonged more to this *mahasiddha* tradition than to that of the rapidly-growing celibate monasticism. He was born near the end of the heyday of the Tibetan *mahasiddha* culture, which with each passing generation became increasingly rare.

3 That said, monasticism did serve the Tibetans well and the monastic institution did produce a considerable number of remarkable personalities, as it continues to do today. Nonetheless, it hardly does tantrism justice, and the more tantra-friendly atmosphere created by Tantric Buddhism entering the world stage promises to lead to many interesting developments.

4 The monastic fever that spread throughout Tibet from roughly the twelfth century onward completely transformed the nature of Tantric Buddhism. Whereas Padma Sambhava was a strong lay yogi, and engaged in considerable *ganachakra* activity in the classical sense, as had Marpa and the early Sakya masters, the tradition was replaced by symbolic gestures as the power of the monkhood grew.

THE TIBETAN BOOK OF THE DEAD AND THE BARDO LITERATURE OF BUDDHIST INDIA

1 The Tibetans consider Vasubandhu's treatise to be Hinayana and Asanga's to be Mahayana. Although the two were brothers, they differed considerably in their philosophical perspectives. It is said that after Asanga completed his twelve-year meditation retreat and released his famous 'Five Treatises of Maitreya', his brother proclaimed, 'My brother does twelve years of meditation and gains no realization, and instead just publishes these fabulous books of fiction and fantasy.'

2 Chakras are the energy centres, *nadis* the energy pathways, and the energies the subtle currents that flow through the pathways.

3 Although the individual Tibetan schools like to think of themselves as very different from one another in substance, in reality they are 99 per cent the same in their ideas and spiritual practices. They mostly just use slightly different linguistics because of the periods in Tibetan history in which each developed, and organize the doctrines and yogas in individual infrastructures.

4 I am sure that some readers will think it inappropriate to link the Tilopa and Naropa lineages to those of Padma Sambhava. However, they were all products of much the same educational system in India. All three had roots in Nalanda Monastery in their shaved-head monk days (before they disrobed and became wild and hairy tantric yogis), and all three were part of the same wave of classical-period Indian Tantric Buddhism.

BARDO, DREAMS, SEX AND DEATH

1 Although the First Dalai Lama did not personally write about these tantric traditions, he taught them on many occasions. His *Collected Works* contain several *zintri* or 'notes' taken by disciples on those occasions. These notes were then edited into books. Sometimes *zintri* also refers to notes that the master himself took at a discourse he attended as a young lama in training. The First Dalai Lama's *Collected Works* only contains the former.

BYPASSING THE BARDO, PURIFICATION IN THE BARDO, AND CARING FOR THE DEAD

1 Karma Lingpa's *Chi Tsen Takpa*, or *Observing Death Omens*, is a classic. My translation of it is included as Chapter Five in one of my earlier books, *Death and Dying: The Tibetan Tradition* (London: Penguin Viking, 1986). This work was later published as *Living in the Face of Death: The Tibetan Tradition* (USA: Snow Lion, 1998).

KARMA LINGPA, THE BARDO TODOL, AND THE TREASURE TEXT TRADITION

1 Chogyam Trungpa was the first to publish the verse in America. Naturally, Americans loved the idea of being mentioned in a prophecy. Buddha also made a similar prophecy that Tibetans often quote. It comes from one of the numerous editions of the *Lankavatara Sutra,* wherein Buddha states,

> 2,500 years after my passing
> My dharma will go to the land of the Red Man.

The year 1956 was recognized internationally as the official 2,500th anniversary of Buddha's passing. That year, Indian Prime Minister Nehru invited masters from all Buddhist traditions of the world to participate in a large memorial celebration in India. This event opened the door to the rebirth of Buddhism in India, which had been badly attacked and oppressed by Muslim occupations. It was also the first time the most high Tibetan lamas came into contact with foreign Buddhists and the international community.

KARMA LINGPA'S PREFACE

1 The Tibetan pronoun *kong* does not indicate any gender. It means he/she. I have followed the English norm of presenting a non-gender as 'he'. Although using he/she might be more accurate, unfortunately it is abrasive to the eye of the reader.

2 In other words, there is no need to perform a reading of *The Tibetan Book of the Dead* for accomplished yogis who have already achieved high realization. They will be able to apply the appropriate yogas and meditations at the time by themselves, without the assistance of a ritualist.

A PRELIMINARY TO THE ACTUAL READING

1 The word *mara* generally refers to an evil spirit, or to death itself. Here it refers to a karmic hindrance, a predisposition of behaviour that creates negative energy and infrastructures.

2 Karma Lingpa's text is divided between his instruction to the ritualist and what the ritualist reads out to the deceased.

POINTING OUT THE BARDO OF TRUTH

1 Karma Lingpa has another work called 'Liberation by Analyzing the Signs of Death', among the 'Liberation Through Hearing in the Bardo' texts, where he explains how a ritualist should recognize the state of the deceased's wandering soul. Its translation has been included in *Death and Dying: The Tibetan Tradition* (London: Penguin Arkana, 1986).

THE BARDO OF WRATHFUL MANIFESTATIONS

1 The Tibetan text provides a description of the mandala deity with the very same words that are used in the standard sadhana of self-invocation as the Mandala of Peaceful and Wrathful Deities, or liturgical text that is chanted daily by an initiate into the system.

Selected Reading

Cuevas, Bryan J. *The Hidden History of The Tibetan book of the Dead.* Oxford: Oxford University Press, 2003.

Dawa-Samdup, Lama Kazi and Dr W.Y. Evans-Wentz, translated, introduced and annotated. *The Tibetan Book of the Dead.* Oxford: Oxford University Press, 1927.

Dorje, Gyurme, trans. *The Tibetan Book of the Dead: The Great Liberation by Hearing in the Intermediate States.* Edited by Graham Coleman with Thupten Jinpa. New York: Viking Publications, 2006.

Fremantle, Francesca and Chogyam Trungpa, translated with commentary. *The Tibetan Book of the Dead: The Great Liberation through Hearing in the Bardo* by Guru Rinpoche according to Karma Lingpa. Boston: Shambhala, 1987.

Govinda, Lama Anagarika. *The Foundations of Tibetan Mysticism.* Maine: Samuel Weiser Books, 1969.

Hodge, Stephen and Martin Boord. *The Illustrated Tibetan Book of the Dead: A New Translation with Commentary*. New York: Sterling Pub. Co., 1999.

Lauf, Detlef Ingo. *Secret Doctrines of The Tibetan Book of the Dead*. Boston and London: Shambhala Publications, 1990.

Leary, Timothy. *The Psychedelic Experience: A Manual Based on The Tibetan Book of the Dead*. New York: University Books, 1964.

MacHovec, Frank J. *The Tibetan Book of the Dead: A Modern English Translation*. New York: Peter Pauper Press, 1972.

Mullin, Glenn H. *Death and Dying: The Tibetan Tradition*. London and Boston: Viking Arkana, 1986.

Mullin, Glenn H. *Living in the Face of Death*. New York: Snow Lion Publications, 1992.

Nairn, Rob. *Living, Dreaming, Dying: Practical Wisdom from The Tibetan Book of the Dead*. Boston: Shambhala Publications, 2004.

Rinpoche, Sogyal. *The Tibetan Book of Living and Dying*. Edited by Patrick Gaffney and Andrew Harvey. California: Harper Publications, 1992.

Thurman, Robert A.F., trans. *The Tibetan Book of the Dead: The Great Book of Natural Liberation through Understanding in the Between*. New York: Bantam Books, 1994.

van Itallie, Jean-Claude. *The Tibetan Book of the Dead for Reading Aloud*. California: North Atlantic Books, 1998.

Following pages: *Devotees come to honour Buddha at his final resting place in Kushinagar, India.*

ISBN: 978-81-7436-436-4

Photo Credits
© John Gilmore Ford Family Collection: Page 49
© Libermann Collection: Page 98
© Zimmerman Family Collection: Page 120
© Thomas Kelly: All other pictures

Published in India by
Roli Books in arrangement with
Roli & Janssen BV, The Netherlands
M-75, Greater Kailash-II Market,
New Delhi 110 048, India.
Phone: ++91-11-4068 2000
Fax: ++91-11-29217185
Email: info@rolibooks.com
Website: rolibooks.com

Editor: Richa Burman
Design: Supriya Saran
Production: Naresh Nigam

Printed and bound in India